MODERN ENGLISH

second edition

MODERN ENGLISH

exercises for non-native speakers

PART I: parts of speech

MARCELLA FRANK

New York University

Prentice Hall Regents   *Englewood Cliffs, New Jersey 07632*

Editorial/production supervision and
    interior design by Anthony Keating and Eva Jaunzems
Cover design by Ben Santora
Manufacturing buyer: Harry P. Baisley

0-13-593831-7 01

Prentice-Hall International (UK) Limited, *London*
Prentice-Hall of Australia Pty. Limited, *Sydney*
Prentice-Hall of Canada, Inc., *Toronto*
Prentice-Hall Hispanoamericana, S.A., *Mexico*
Prentice-Hall of India Private Limited, *New Delhi*
Prentice-Hall of Japan, Inc., *Tokyo*
Prentice-Hall of Southeast Asia Pte. Ltd., *Singapore*
Editora Prentice-Hall do Brasil, Ltda., *Rio de Janeiro*
Whitehall Books Limited, *Wellington, New Zealand*

CONTENTS

4

AUXILIARIES **95**

5

ADJECTIVES 131

Preface
to the Second Edition

This new edition of *Modern English: Exercises for Non-native Speakers* retains the format of the first edition. The teacher will find the same carefully presented exercises that offer a wide range of practice in a systematic manner. Most of the exercises from the first edition have been kept, but some have been shortened to make room for others that are equally useful. I have replaced or revised sentences that were not clearcut examples of the usage being studied or that teachers found objectionable or outdated. Also, I have tried to clarify some of the explanations and instructions. Finally, I have omitted the summarizing exercises at the end of each chapter in Part Two.

This second edition has several new features that should increase its usefulness.

1. Reviews have been added to the texts:
   To Part One, a review for each chapter. Review sentences have been taken mainly from the sentences already in the chapter. These reviews can also be used as tests.
   To Part Two, a final review section of all the structures in Part Two. Each exercise in this section gives practice in combining sentences to produce several possible structures rather than just one structure. Students have the chance here to see which grammatical structures are available for the same meaning. Integrated within this practice are the punctuation, position, variety of usage, or possible omission of some structure words.

2. Objective tests have been added to both Part I and Part II. The test items in Part One cover mainly the structures practiced in this part. In Part Two, the test items include structures studied in both volumes.

3. In Part Two, a brief section has been added to give students help in preparing for the TOEFL test. This section covers problems in agreement and number, fragments and run-on sentences, verb tenses, verbals, word forms, word order, prepositions and conjunctions, articles, comparison, parallelism, repetition.

4. The instructor's manual that accompanies this second edition has been expanded to give not only the complete answers to the exercises but also abundant guidance to teachers using the books. There are further explanations of some of the structures, and suggestions on how to introduce the practice on many of the structures, as well as how to use some of them in communicative situations.

5. The answers have been set up in the manual in such a way that they can be reproduced for use by students for self-study.

Students who use these workbooks have available to them two of my reference books. Advanced students can get reference information from *Modern English: A Practical Reference Guide*. (Prentice-Hall, Englewood Cliffs, N.J., 1972). Less advanced students can refer to my recently published *Writer's Companion* (Prentice-Hall, Englewood Cliffs, N.J., 1983), a small, compact guide to usage and writing.

At this time, I wish to express my appreciation to Robin Baliszewski, Brenda White, and Eva Jaunzems of Prentice-Hall, Inc. for their great help in seeing this second edition through to completion.

Marcella Frank
New York, New York

Preface
to the First Edition

The purpose of the two volumes of *Modern English: Exercises for Non-native Speakers* is to provide advanced students of English as a foreign language with much carefully controlled and integrated practice on points of usage that continue to trouble such students. While the emphasis of these exercises is on written work, many of them may be used for oral drill as well.

The exercises are arranged systematically for ease of location. They progress from the less difficult to the more difficult, from strict control to looser control. Explanations are kept to a minimum; students understand what they are to do from the examples, many of which are given in contrast.

It would be desirable to use the workbooks in conjunction with *Modern English: A Practical Reference Guide* (Prentice-Hall, Englewood Cliffs, N.J., 1972), which describes in detail the facts of usage on which the practice in the workbooks is based. However, the exercises have been set up so that the workbooks can be used independently of the reference guide.

The chapters in the workbooks are correlated with the chapters in the reference book. Thus, the sequence of practice moves from usage connected with the parts of speech to usage connected with the complex syntactic structures. As in the reference guide, the chapters on parts of speech have been influenced by structural grammar, those in complex syntactic structures by transformational grammar.

PART I:
PARTS OF SPEECH

Each chapter on a part of speech begins with a chart outlining the structural features of the part of speech (function, position, form, markers). This outline is based on the description in *MODERN ENGLISH: A Practical Reference Guide*. Then come many exercises on word forms (inflectional and derivational suffixes, spelling peculiarities and irregularities), word order and other troublesome usages connected wtih each part of speech.

PART II:
SENTENCES AND COMPLEX STRUCTURES

The complex structures that have been chosen for practice are those derived from simple basic sentences. Mastery of these structures is especially important for writing since they provide grammatical shapes for the expression of predications and thus relate grammar to meaning. The structures that are included are clauses, verbals, abstract noun phrases, and appositive phrases.

Each chapter on the complex structures is introduced by a chart that illustrates the various types of the structure. This is followed by transformational exercises involving: a) changes from the basic subject-verb-complement; b) the position(s) of the structure; c) the punctuation of the structure; d) substitutions for the structure; e) abridgment of the structure. At the end of each chapter is an exercise requiring a one-sentence summary of a paragraph.

I wish to acknowledge my special indebtedness to Milton G. Saltzer, Associate Director of the American Language Institute, New York University, for making it possible for me to try out a preliminary edition of these workbooks for several semesters at our Institute. Thanks are also due to my colleagues for their useful suggestions and comments, and to the students of the American Language Institute for helping me see which exercises needed improvement or change.

M.F.

1
Nouns

STRUCTURAL DESCRIPTION OF NOUNS

Function	Sentences	Position
1. subject of verb	*John loves Mary.*	before the verb
2. object of verb		after the verb
a. direct object	*John loves **Mary**.*	
b. indirect object	*John sent **Mary** money.*	
c. retained object	*Mary was sent some **money**.*	
3. object of preposition	*I took it from **John**.*	after a preposition
4. complement		after the verb
a. subjective (after verbs like **be**)	*John is the **president**.*	
b. objective	*They elected John **president**.*	
5. noun adjunct	*John waited at the **bus** stop.*	before a noun
6. appositive	*John, **president** of his club, gave a speech.*	after a noun
7. direct address	***John**, come here.*	usually at the beginning of the sentence

Form		Markers
Inflectional Endings *-s* for plural *'s* or *s'* for possessive	Derivational Endings -ment; -ion; -a(e)nce; -ure; -age; -th; -ness; -hood; -ship; -ity; -ing for a person *who:* -er; -or; -ist; -ant; -ian	Determiners: *The* _____ (articles) *My* _____ (possessives) *This* _____ (demonstratives) *Four* _____ (numbers) *Some* _____ (indefinite pronouns) Descriptive adjectives: *Large* _____ Prepositions: *In* _____ Other nouns: *Bus* _____

A noun is often the head word of the grammatical structure in which it appears.

Subject

*The **house** on the corner belongs to my uncle.*
(**House** is the head word of the entire subject **the house on the corner**.)

Object of verb:
  direct object

*My husband sells expensive Chinese **antiques**.*
(**Antiques** is the head word of the direct object **expensive Chinese antiques**.)

  indirect object

*My uncle sold that rich **couple** some expensive antiques.*
(**Couple** is the head word of the indirect object **that rich couple**. Indirect objects are used after verbs such as **bring, buy, give, make, owe, pay, sell, send, teach, write**.)

Object of preposition:
(in a prepositional
phrase)

*The price of those **antiques** is very high.*
(**Antiques** is the head word of the object of the preposition **those antiques**. Some common prepositions are **in, of, on, at, by, for, about, from, to, after**.)

Complement:[1]
  subjective
  complement

*My uncle is the richest **man** in town.*
(**Man** is the head word of the subjective complement **the richest man in town**. Subjective complements appear after verbs like **be, seem, appear, remain, become**.)

  objective
  complement

*I consider my uncle a very fortunate **man**.*
(**Man** is the head word of the objective complement **a very fortunate man**. Objective complements are used after verbs such as **appoint, consider, elect, name, nominate, select, choose**.)

Underline each noun in the following sentences and write its function above it—subject, direct or indirect object of verb, object of preposition, subjective or objective complement. Use the abbreviations **S, DO, IO, OP, SC, OC**.

EXAMPLE: The children in that family have bad manners.

              S   OP   DO
  The <u>children</u> in that <u>family</u> have bad <u>manners</u>.

1. The customer sent the store a letter complaining about the service.

2. Her daughter was the only student in the school who won a prize.

3. The first President of the United States was George Washington.

4. The American people elected George Washington President.

---

[1]The word *complement,* in its broadest sense, also includes the object of the verb. In its narrowest sense it refers to the subjective complement only. A noun used as a subjective complement is also called a predicate noun.

5. The old man paid the boy some money for the newspaper.

6. The company considers Mr. Jones the best man for the job.

7. Her son became a famous musician because of her encouragement.

1-2
PLURAL FORMS OF NOUNS

Nouns are usually made plural by the addition of *s*. A number of nouns have other plural forms.

---

1. *es plural*
   a. nouns ending in sibilant sounds spelled with *s, z, ch, sh, x* — **classes, churches, dishes, boxes** *but* **monarchs** (*ch* spells a [k] sound)
   b. nouns ending in *y* preceded by a consonant: *y* is changed to *i* — **ladies, countries, boundaries** *but* **toys, keys** (*y* is preceded by a vowel)
   c. one-syllable nouns ending in a single *f* or *fe:* *f* is changed to *v* — **leaves, thieves, knives** *but* **sheriffs, staffs, beliefs, chiefs** Some words may also have a regular plural— **scarfs** *or* **scarves, dwarfs** *or* **dwarves.**
   d. nouns ending in *o:*
      es only — **Negroes, heroes, echoes, potatoes, tomatoes, embargoes**
      s only — terms in music—**pianos, sopranos** *o* preceded by a vowel—**cameos, radios** others—**photos, zeros**
      es or *s* — **cargoes** *or* **cargos, volcanoes** *or* **volcanos, mulattoes** *or* **mulattos**

2. *other types of plural*
   a. *-en* ending — **children, oxen, brethren**[2]
   b. internal vowel change — **teeth, mice, men**
   c. no change — **deer, sheep, series**

Write the plural for the following nouns. Use the dictionary when necessary.

apology _____   fox _____

businessman _____   mosquito _____

sheep _____   torch _____

bush _____   embargo _____

Negro _____   species _____

quantity _____   story _____

[2]An older plural for **brother,** now used mainly in religious or literary contexts.

tariff _____   roof _____

dash _____   quiz _____

attorney _____   supply _____

hero _____   epoch _____

wharf _____   studio _____

valley _____   bus _____

means _____   fallacy _____

thief _____   wife _____

volcano _____   arch _____

1-3
FOREIGN PLURALS OF NOUNS

Singular Ending	Plural Ending	
-us	-i	stimulus—stimuli, radius—radii
-a	-ae	larva—larvae, vertebra—vertebrae
-um*	-a	memorandum—memoranda, stratum—strata
-is	-es	crisis—crises, parenthesis—parentheses
-on*	-a	criterion—criteria, phenomenon—phenomena
-ex, -ix	-ices	vortex—vortices, matrix—matrices

*There is a tendency for foreign words adopted in English to develop regular plural forms. Thus dictionaries now also give **memorandums, criterions**.

Write the plurals of these foreign words that have been taken over into the English language. Note which of these words also have regular plural endings. Use the dictionary when necessary.

criterion _____   minutia _____

axis _____   stratum _____

alumna _____   cactus _____

alumnus _____   nebula _____

diagnosis _____   stimulus _____

datum[3] _____   bacterium[3] _____

index _____   vertebra _____

[3]These words are rarely used in the singular.

nucleus _____   syllabus _____

thesis _____   focus _____

formula _____   appendix _____

hypothesis _____   emphasis _____

1-4
INFLECTED POSSESSIVE FORMS

1. Use **'s** for all nouns not ending in **s**.
   a. *singular nouns*—The **girl's** dress is expensive.
   b. *irregular plurals of nouns*—The **children's** dresses are expensive.
2. Use **'** for all nouns already ending in **s**.
   a. *plural nouns*—The **girls'** dresses are expensive.
   b. *singular nouns, especially proper nouns*—**Dickens'** (also **Dickens's**) novels are excellent.
3. Use **'s** at the end of a group of nouns—The **Queen of England's** throne; the **boy from Canada's** mother.

The inflected possessive form is generally preferred for words referring to animate beings, the **of** phrase for words signifying things or ideas. However, the inflected form may also be used with nouns that represent: time (**a day's journey**), natural phenomena (**the earth's atmosphere**), political entities (**Japan's industrialization**), **groups** of people working together (**the company's new refinery**).

Change the **of** phrases in the following sentences to inflected possessive forms.

EXAMPLE: a. The parents *of the students* were invited to the graduation.
   The students' parents were invited to the graduation.

   b. It has always been the policy *of this newspaper* to report the news honestly and accurately.
   It has always been this newspaper's policy to report the news honestly and accurately.

1. The house *of Mr. Jones* has recently been sold.

_____

2. The crew *of the ship* decided to go on strike.

_____

3. He was irritated by the attitude *of his friends*.

_____

4. The rays *of the sun* shine on all.

_____

5. The courteous service *of the waiters* pleased all the guests in the restaurant.

_____

6.   The doctor is waiting for the report *of the X-ray technician*.

_____

7.   The distance *of the earth* from the moon is now known.

_____

8.   The willingness *of the two countries* to negotiate their differences may help to avoid bloodshed.

_____

_____

9.   The reputation *of this railroad* for safety and reliability has brought about its prosperity.

_____

_____

10. The hair *of the baby* is becoming lighter.

_____

11. The garden *of our next-door neighbors* is more beautiful than ours.

_____

_____

1-5
COUNTABLE vs. NONCOUNTABLE NOUNS

Some nouns are not used in the plural. Such noncountable nouns may be:

1.   *mass nouns* (representing concrete objects in their undivided form)
     a.   foods—**sugar, coffee, milk, chicken, meat, fish**
     b.   Metals, minerals, gases, etc.—**gold, iron, coal, oil, oxygen, sulphur**
2.   *abstract nouns* (including fields of study, sports)—**democracy, beauty, philosophy, chemistry, tennis.**

Examples of other nouns which are not used in the plural are: clothing, equipment, housework, information, machinery, slang.

A. Add -s to the countable nouns that can be made plural.

information _____   vegetation _____

literature _____   youngster _____

vocabulary _____   lumber _____

advertising _____   stationery _____

advertisement _____   luggage _____

climate _____   laughter _____

homework _____   traffic _____

assignment _____   knowledge _____

slang _____   advice _____

weather _____   scenery _____

clothing _____   architect _____

machinery _____   engineering _____

machine _____   architecture _____

propaganda _____   skyscraper _____

equipment _____   committee _____

B. Some nouns may have either a countable or a noncountable sense.

    1. In their countable use, the nouns refer to individuals in a group rather than to the group itself.
        There were many *chickens* **in the yard.** (**Chickens** refers to the individual birds.)
        vs. **They eat** *chicken* **very often.** (**Chicken** is considered in the mass—as one undivided item of food.)

    2. The nouns used in a countable sense have the meaning of *a kind of, a type of.*
        The two most common *metals* **for kitchen utensils are aluminum and stainless steel.** (**Metals** implies *kinds of*.)
        vs. **Most kitchen utensils are made of** *metal*.

Use a noncountable singular noun or a countable plural noun. Do not use an article with a singular noncountable noun.

EXAMPLE: a. It has been said that (youth) <u>youth</u> is wasted on young people.

          b. Several (youth) <u>youths</u> were loitering in the schoolyard.

    1. The most expensive wigs are made of human (hair) _____.

    2. He is so bald that we can almost count the (hair) _____ on his head.

    3. Various (fruit) _____ were on display at the fair.

    4. Let's have some (fruit) _____ for dessert.

    5. He has always been praised for his great (strength) _____ of

        (character) _____.

6. One of his great (strength)[4] _____ is his ability to get along with people.

7. He doesn't like to drink (wine) _____ or (beer) _____.

8. France produces many (wine) _____ in her various regions.

9. That company will not hire you unless you have (experience) _____.

10. He spoke about one of the most interesting (experience) _____ he had had overseas.

1-6
DERIVATION (1)
ADDING AGENT-DENOTING SUFFIXES

Add noun suffixes to the following. Make whatever changes are necessary.

A. Suffixes that mean a person who _____ *-s:*
   (Use *-or, -er, -ist, -ent*)

collect _____   discover _____

depend _____   invent _____

employ _____   sail _____

perform _____   tour _____

supply _____   farm _____

visit _____   reside _____

type _____   manage _____

conquer _____   advise _____

B. Suffixes that mean a person who is active in (or engages in) the field of _____.
   (Use *-ian, -ist, -eon, -er, -eer*)

biology _____   dentistry _____

music _____   engineering _____

chemistry _____   optometry _____

[4]The noun in an *of* phrase following *one* is plural.

physics _____   auctioning _____

surgery _____   statistics _____

economics _____   law _____

1-7
DERIVATION (2)
DOUBLING FINAL CONSONANTS
BEFORE NOUN SUFFIXES

one-syllable word			rób	b	er
two-syllable word		oc	cúr	r	ence
	but	préf	er		ence

Note that: (1) the added noun suffix *begins with a vowel;* (2) the syllable before the noun suffix *ends in a single consonant preceded by a single vowel;* (3) the syllable before the added noun suffix *is stressed.*

Use the correct form of the noun.

1. The (propel) _____ of the plane was damaged.

2. Venus is the (god) _____ of love.

3. They had a large (wed) _____.

4. The (begin) _____ of the book is interesting.

5. He removed the (wrap) _____ from the candy bar.

6. We are writing in (refer) _____ to your letter of June 18.

7. There were many (beg) _____ on the road.

8. An (occur) _____ such as this was completely unexpected.

9. They traveled with very little (bag) _____.

10. This ball is made of (rub) _____.

11. There is a great (differ) _____ between the two brothers.

12. The chief argument for capital punishment is that it acts as a (deter) _____ to crime.

13. I'll ask the (drug) _____ what to take for my cold.

14. The police are taking measures to prevent the (recur) _____ of any violence by the strikers.

15. The (commit) _____ is deliberating that matter now.

1-8
DERIVATION (3)
ADDING NOUN SUFFIXES
TO WORDS THAT END IN SILENT *E*

1. **Keep the *e* before a consonant**

arrangement	Exceptions:	judgment[5]	wisdom
rudeness		acknowledgment[5]	truth[6]
statehood		abridgment[5]	width[6]
		argument[5]	

2. **Drop the *e* before a vowel**

   purity
   creation
   pleasure

Add the noun suffixes to the words given below. Make whatever changes are necessary.

associate + ion _____

advertise + ment _____

expose + ure _____

civilize + ation _____

judge + ment _____

interfere + ence _____

retire + ment _____

responsible + ity _____

receive + t (irregular) _____

arrive + al _____

twelve + th (irregular) _____

enclose + ure _____

encourage + ment _____

wide + th _____

operate + ion _____

idle + ness _____

seize + ure _____

compare + ison _____

polite + ness _____

argue + ment _____

safe + ty _____

hostile + ity _____

1-9
DERIVATION (4)
CHANGING *Y* TO *I*
BEFORE A CONSONANT OR A VOWEL

y before a vowel: carriage   *y* before a consonant: happiness
                      supplier   loneliness
                      alliance   classification

---

[5]In British English, these words keep the *e*.
[6] The *e* is usually dropped before *th.*

Add the noun suffixes to the words given below. Make whatever changes are necessary.

bury + al _____   vary + ety _____

apply + cation _____   lovely + ness _____

marry + age _____   lively + hood _____

try + al _____   lazy + ness _____

holy + day _____   likely + hood _____

handy + man (exception)[7] _____   busy + ness _____

1-10
DERIVATION (5)
CHANGING THE STEM BEFORE NOUN SUFFIXES

Fill in the blanks with the appropriate noun forms. Because the first part of each of the words in this exercise changes when the noun suffix is added, you may need the help of a dictionary.

Nouns from Verbs

1. The (maintain) _____ of that building is the responsibility of Mr. Jones.

2. He gave a vivid (describe) _____ of his home town.

3. The child was punished for his (disobey) _____.

4. His (succeed) _____ in business was the result of hard work.

5. Everyone would like a (reduce) _____ in taxes.

6. We must find a (solve) _____ to this problem.

7. His wife's constant (suspect) _____ of infidelity irritated him.

8. The judge's (decide) _____ is final.

9. The tornado caused a great deal of (destroy) _____.

10. That gas can easily cause an (explode) _____.

11. What is the (pronounce) _____ of this word?

12. The (omit) _____ of a few words in the contract caused a great deal of trouble.

[7]The *y* is kept before endings that form compounds, such as *-man* (laundryman), *-side* (countryside).

13. A (compare) _____ between the two systems reveals that one is much more efficient than the other.

14. For a long time people had many (misconceive) _____ about the nature of mental disorders.

15. He couldn't give a satisfactory (explain) _____ for his absence.

16. The (conquer) _____ of England by the Normans occurred in 1066.

Nouns from Adjectives

1. Cats have a lot of (curious) _____.

2. What is the (deep) _____, the (high) _____ and the (long) _____ of this box?

3. Although he was a world-renowned scientist, he always behaved with (humble) _____.

4. He has great (strong) _____ and (noble) _____ of character.

5. She was thanked for her (generous) _____.

6. The government is trying to help those who live in (poor) _____.

1-11
DERIVATION (6)
CHANGING VERBS OR ADJECTIVES TO NOUNS

Fill in the noun form that is required because of the preceding italicized word.

EXAMPLE: He was greatly *attracted* by wealth, an <u>attraction</u> which grew with the passing of years.

1. He soon became *acquainted* with the mayor, an _____ which brought him many political benefits.

2. The young boy was *grateful* to the judge for his leniency. His _____ took the form of helping other youngsters to obey the law.

3. He was *not certain* that his farm could continue to be profitable. Because of this _____ he decided to sell the farm.

4. He was always severely *critical* of his wife. Finally his wife left him when she could no

   longer stand his _____ .

5. Their father was *partial* to the youngest daughter, a _____
   that distressed the other children.

6. Many of the citizens were *indignant* because of the increase in taxes. They expressed

   their _____ by sending a lengthy petition to the mayor.

7. There is a saying that gentlemen *prefer* blondes. This _____
   is probably not true for all gentlemen.

8. She always felt *inferior* to her beautiful sister. This feeling of

   _____ caused her to be shy and retiring.

9. Marcel Proust *remembered* many incidents of his childhood. This

   _____ of the past was all minutely recorded in his novels.

10. The wealthy young man decided to *renounce* his life of ease and become a hermit. This

    _____ of his former way of life surprised all his friends.

11. No one may *enter* through this gate. The _____ to the park
    is around the corner.

12. The heavy pack he was carrying *hindered* his movements. The camper decided that the

    next time he would take along nothing that would be such a _____
    to him.

13. He *injured* his foot while climbing. This _____ prevented
    him from going any further.

1-12
NOUN COMPOUNDS

Two nouns may be joined together to form one vocabulary unit (**gasoline station, dining room**). In such noun compounds, the first noun narrows down the scope of the second noun; thus, the word **gasoline** limits the more general word **station** to the one particular place where gasoline is sold.

Noun compounds may be written as two separate words—especially if both parts are long—as hyphenated words, or as single words. For some longer combinations, the American preference is for two separate words (**evening gown**), while the British preference is for hyphenated words (**evening-gown**).

Nouns may also be compounded with prepositions (**makeup**), with adjectives (**common sense**) and with prepositional phrases (**son-in-law**).

Make noun compounds out of the following phrases. If necessary, check the dictionary to see whether the two parts of the words are written as one word, with or without a hyphen, or as separate words.

EXAMPLES: a. a book about grammar <u>a grammar book</u>

   b. the end of the week <u>the weekend *or* the week-end</u>

1.   a room for dining _____

2.   a store that sells drugs _____

3.   a bomb powered by atomic energy _____

4.   a salesman who travels _____

5.   the lids that cover the eyes _____

6.   a board for ironing clothes _____

7.   a person who keeps books _____

8.   gum for chewing _____

9.   a store that sells hardware _____

10.   seeing the sights _____

11.   control of birth _____

12.   stew with lamb _____

13.   production of steel _____

14.   a person who tends bar _____

15.   a person who witnesses a scene with his or her own eyes

   _____

16.   a store that sells books _____

17.   a gown worn at night for sleeping _____

18.   checks for travelers _____

19.   a mine of gold _____

20.   a carriage for a baby _____

1-13
AGREEMENT WITH VERBS (1)

The verb must agree in number with the subject.

The **girl is** resting.
The **girls are** resting.

If the subject includes modifiers, the verb agrees with the noun head in the subject.

His **technique** for solving crimes **is** very simple.
The **advertisements** in the front part of a newspaper **are** usually the most expensive.

A noncountable noun used as a subject requires a singular verb.

His baggage was lost yesterday (*vs.* His **bags were** lost yesterday.)
This information is correct. (*vs.* These **facts are** correct.)

A collective noun used as a subject generally occurs with a single verb in American English, unless emphasis is placed on the individual members of the collective unit.[8]

The committee has been preparing a new proposal.
but **The committee have disagreed among themselves about the terms of the proposal.**

Put parentheses around the entire subject of each sentence, and underline the word that the verb agrees with. Then fill in the proper form of the verb. *Use only the present tense.*

EXAMPLE: a. (The <u>rays</u> of the sun) [shine] <u>shine</u> on all.

b. (A little <u>knowledge</u>) [be] <u>is</u> a dangerous thing.

1. The amount of space between the lines (depend) _____ on the size of the story.

2. His method of doing things (be) _____ always admirable.

3. The choir (practice) _____ twice a week.

4. An overuse of slang words (mark) _____ a person as uneducated.

5. Some members of the committee (be) _____ absent.

6. The public (be) _____ invited to attend the meeting.

7. Many people on the ship (be) _____ getting seasick from the violent waves.

8. The singing of the birds (awaken) _____ me every morning.

9. The police[9] (be) _____ patrolling the area very carefully.

10. The clothing on these racks (be) _____ being put on sale tomorrow.

11. The front page articles in that newspaper usually (consist)

_____ of news about international events.

12. No frozen poultry (be) _____ sold in this store.

13. A sound knowledge of mathematics (be) _____ required for this kind of work.

[8]Collective nouns refer to people or animals in a group: the public, a family, an audience, a jury, an orchestra, a team.
[9]The word *police* is always plural.

14. The number of people who understand Einstein's theory of relativity (be)

_____ very small.[10]

15. A number of people (be) _____ waiting at the airport to greet the movie star.

16. The spirit in which these things are done (be) _____ very important.

17. The people who live in this building (seem) _____ very friendly.

1-14
AGREEMENT WITH VERBS (2)
NOUNS ENDING IN S

Some nouns ending in *s* may cause problems in agreement.

1. Some are singular noncountable nouns—**news, billiards, economics** (name of a field of study)

> **The news about the increase in jobs is good.**
> **Physics is a difficult, but fascinating, subject.**

The name used for a field of study may be plural if it refers to a practical matter.

> **The acoustics in this room are not good.**

2. Some nouns have the same form for *singular or plural*—**series, means, species.**
3. Some nouns are plural only and require *plural verbs*—**brains, riches, goods, clothes, premises, proceeds.** Included in this group of plurals are nouns signifying two-part objects—**scissors, trousers, eyeglasses.**
4. Some nouns may be *singular or plural*—**headquarters, barracks, measles** (name of a disease).
5. Nouns representing quantities and amounts that are considered as one unit are usually *singular*—**five dollars, three quarts.**

> **Five dollars is too much to pay for that pen.**

Underline the correct form of the verb. Consult the dictionary in case of doubt about whether the noun ending in *s* is singular or plural.

1. Mathematics (has, have) never been my favorite subject.
2. The news printed in that paper (is, are) never accurate.
3. A second series of books on American literature (is, are) being planned by the publisher.
4. Several means of accomplishing our purpose (was, were) proposed at our meeting.

[10]**The number** is usually singular, **a number** is plural.

5. The scissors (was, were) here a few minutes ago.
6. Over $1,500 (has, have) already been withheld from his salary for federal income taxes.
7. Billiards (is, are) his favorite game.
8. Two gallons of paint (is, are) all we need.
9. The goods (was, were) shipped yesterday.
10. Athletics (has, have) always been emphasized in this school.
11. The mumps (causes, cause) a swelling in the glands below the ears.
12. The proceeds of the sale (is, are) going to charity.
13. Ten minutes (is, are) too short a time to finish this test.
14. The premises of the school (has, have) been cleared of students because of a bomb threat.
15. His ethics in that business deal (is, are) being questioned by some financial experts.
16. Her clothes (is, are) always in the latest style.

1-15
AGREEMENT WITH VERBS (3)
NOUNS FROM ADJECTIVES

Adjectives used as nouns often refer to a group of persons and require a plural verb. Such adjective forms are usually preceded by **the.**

The Irish produce some fine crystalware.
The rich get richer, while the poor get poorer.

Change each of the phrases beginning with **those who** to **the** + **an adjective.** Then supply the correct form of the verb **be.**

EXAMPLE: Those who were seriously wounded (past) immediately taken to the hospital.

The seriously wounded were immediately taken to the hospital.

(Note that an adjective used as a noun may retain its adverbial modifier—*seriously*.)

1. *Those who are aged* (present) now being provided with cheap or free medical care.

_____

2. *Those who are young* (present) often very impatient with their elders.

_____

3. *Those who are needy* (present) now receiving enough to live on.

_____

4. *Those who are unemployed* (present) entitled to apply for unemployment insurance.

_____

5. Only *those who were very prominent* (past) invited to the reception for the ambassador.

_____

6. After the terrible landslide that destroyed the village, *those who were living* (past) removed at once, *those who were dead* (past) left behind.

_____

_____

7. In this school, *those who are blind* (present) being taught Braille, *those who are deaf* (present) being taught how to speak.

_____

_____

8. *Those who were the most aggressive among the strikers* (past) in favor of prolonging the strike.

_____

9. *Those who are socially acceptable* (present) the only ones who are ever invited to their home.

_____

REVIEW OF NOUNS

A. Write the plural of the following nouns. (Some words have the same form.) Write *no plural* for those words which are not used in the plural.

boundary _____   quantity _____

belief _____   box _____

information _____   luggage _____

potato _____   attorney _____

crisis _____   wife _____

child _____   analysis _____

homework _____   supply _____

species _____   advice _____

stimulus _____   church _____

quiz _____   criterion _____

deer _____   volcano _____

B. Add the noun suffixes, making whatever changes are necessary.

begin + ing _____   wide + th _____

advertise + ment _____   argue + ment _____

expose + ure _____   hostile + ity _____

try + al _____   likely + hood _____

drug + ist _____   commit + ee _____

responsible + ity _____   receive + t _____

vary + ety _____   safe + ty _____

occur + ence _____   busy + ness _____

C. Use the correct form of the noun in parentheses.

1. The (students) _____ parents were invited to the graduation.

2. He was irritated by his (friends) _____ attitude.

3. The (baby) _____ hair is becoming lighter.

4. The most expensive wigs are made of human (hair) _____.

5. Various (fruit) _____ were on display at the fair.

6. One of his great (strength) _____ is his ability to get along with people.

7. His wife's constant (suspect) _____ of infidelity irritated him.

8. The (omit) _____ of a few words in the contract caused a great deal of trouble.

9. He couldn't give a satisfactory (explain) _____ for his answer.

10. The (conquer) _____ of England by the Normans occurred in 1066.

11. What is the (deep) _____, the (high)

    _____ and the (long) _____ of this box?

12. She was thanked for her great (generous) _____.

D. Use the correct form of the verb in parentheses. Use the present tense unless there is a time word that requires the past tense.

1. Many people on the ship (be) _____ getting seasick from the violent waves.

2. The police (be) _____ patrolling that area very carefully.

3. No frozen poultry (be) _____ sold in this store.

4. The news printed in that paper (be) _____ never accurate.

5. The scissors (be) _____ here a few minutes ago.

6. Athletics (be) _____ emphasized in this school.

7. The proceeds of the sale (be) _____ going to charity.

8. The young (be) _____ often very impatient with their elders.

9. The needy (be) _____ now receiving enough to live on.

10. The goods (be) _____ shipped yesterday.

11. The clothing on these racks (be) _____ being put on sale tomorrow.

12. A number of people (be) _____ waiting at the airport to greet the movie star.

2

Pronouns

STRUCTURAL DESCRIPTION OF PRONOUNS

Function and Position	Inflectional Form				
	Personal Pronouns				
Similar to those of nouns. See p. 1.	*Subject*	*Object*	*Possessive Adjective*	*Possessive Pronoun*	*Reflexive*
	I	me	my	mine	myself
	you (s.)	you	your	yours	yourself
	he	him	his	his	himself
	she	her	her	hers	herself
	it	it	its		itself
	we	us	our	ours	ourselves
	you (pl.)	you	your	yours	yourselves
	they	them	their	theirs	themselves

impersonal reflexive—oneself *or* one's self

Interrogative and Relative Pronouns

who	whom	whose	whose

Demonstrative Pronouns

	Singular	*Plural*
	this	these
	that	those

Note that the possessive forms of personal pronouns are written without an apostrophe (**its, ours,** etc.).

Types of Pronouns

1. Personal—**I, you, he, she, it, we, they**

2. Interrogative—**who** (for a person), **what** (for a thing), **which** (for a choice of a person or a thing)

3. Relative—**who** (for a person), **which** (for a thing), **that** (for a person or a thing)

4. Demonstrative—**this, that, such, so**

5. Reflexive—compounds of personal pronouns plus **-self**

6. Indefinite:
   a. person or things—compounds of **some-, any-, no-,** *or* **every-** *plus* **-body, -one, -thing**
   b. quantity—**some, any, several, much,** etc.
   (Personal, relative, demonstrative, reflexive pronouns refer back to nouns previously mentioned.)

7. Expletive—**it, there** (These words fill subject position. The actual subject comes after the verb.)

2-1
FORM OF PERSONAL PRONOUNS

Use the correct form of the pronoun in parentheses. Give the function of each pronoun—subject (**S**), subjective complement (**SC**), object of verb—direct or indirect (**OV**), object of preposition (**OP**).

EXAMPLE: a. John and (I) <u>I</u> are the same age. <u>S</u>

b. The only two who were absent were John and (I) <u>I</u> <u>SC</u> (after the verb **be**) (informally, **me** is used)

c. Our teacher praised John and (I) <u>me</u>. <u>OV</u>

d. The letter was addressed to John and (I) <u>me</u>. <u>OP</u>

1. The money was given to (he) _____ and (I)

   _____. _____

2. Their mother is taking (they) _____ all to the circus.

   _____

3. Everyone finished the test except (I) _____.

   _____

4. All of (they) _____ came late.

   _____

5. My sister and (I) _____ are arriving on the early train.

   _____

6. Between (you) _____ and (I)

   _____, she's not very happy in her new home.

   _____ _____

7. It was (I) _____ who planned this meeting.

   _____

8. Hello, may I speak to Mrs. Jones? This is (she) _____.

   _____

9. They wanted only Robert and (I) _____.

   _____

10. (She) _____ and her sister are planning to give a dinner

    party together. _____

11. Who's at the door? It's (I) _____.[1]

    _____

12. Our neighbors have invited my wife and (I) _____ to their
    New Year's Eve party.

2-2
POSSESSIVE FORMS OF PRONOUNS

Supply one of the possessive forms of the personal pronouns or of **who**. Be careful not to write an apostrophe with any of these pronouns.

EXAMPLE: a. He didn't bring a coat, so I lent him (I) <u>mine</u>.

           b. The store is opening (it) <u>its</u> doors one hour earlier today.

           c. (Who) <u>Whose</u> book is this? I don't know (who) <u>whose</u> book it is.

1. The cat caught (it) _____ tail in the door.[2]

2. In (who) _____ house will the meeting be held?

3. Every nation has (it) _____ own special problems.

4. Can you tell me which house is (they) _____ ?

5. The earth rotates around (it) _____ axis every 24 hours.

6. I don't remember whether the pen I borrowed is (he) _____

   or (she) _____.

---

[1]Although formal usage requires subject form for such a subjective complement, the object form is much more common in informal speech.
[2]The forms of **he** and **she** are also often used for pets.

7. Whether the fault is (they) _____ or (we)

_____, we must correct it immediately.

8. The man (who) _____ car was stolen went to the police immediately.

9. Here are some papers. (Who) _____ are they? Are they (you)

_____?

10. Those noisy children are (we) _____.

11. (Who) _____ money was used to finance the deal?

2-3
DOUBLE POSSESSIVE CONSTRUCTIONS
WITH PRONOUNS

Personal pronouns may appear in double possessive constructions beginning with **of** and ending with the possessive pronoun forms. Such constructions usually have indefinite reference—often meaning **one** (or **some**) among others (an old hat of **yours**). But they may sometimes have definite reference, especially with **that** (**that** new computer of mine).

Use a double possessive construction for the pronouns in parentheses.

EXAMPLE: a. He is a good friend (I) <u>of mine</u>.

b. Some students (she) <u>of hers</u> were on a TV discussion program.

c. That car (they) <u>of theirs</u> always gave them trouble.

1. Any friend (you) _____ is a friend (I)

_____.

2. An old classmate (he) _____ is coming to dinner.

3. A neighbor (we) _____ likes to gossip a great deal.

4. I can understand why they're so proud of that son (they)

_____.

5. A good customer (she) _____ died recently.

6. Some papers (you) _____ got mixed in with some notes (I)

_____.

7. Very few friends (they) _____ were invited to the wedding.

8. Many patients (he) _____ stopped coming to him after he raised his fees.

9. Those jade carvings (they) _____ are worth a fortune.

10. Some neighbors (I) _____ are going on a tour to Europe.

WHO vs. *WHOM*

Who is the subject form, **whom** the object form. (In informal usage, **who** is often also used for the object of a verb.)

Who or **whom** appears in direct questions, in indirect questions (noun clauses), and in adjective clauses.

In the following exercises, supply **who** or **whom**. Label each pronoun you have filled in—Subject (**s**), Object of Verb (**ov**), Object of Preposition (**op**). For this exercise, observe *formal usage,* but note the informal alternatives.

Direct Questions

EXAMPLE: a. <u>Who</u> is watering the plants? <u>s</u> (of **is watering**)

            b. <u>Whom</u> do you want? <u>ov</u> (of **do want**) (Informal, Who do you want?)

            c. From <u>whom</u> did he get the money? <u>op</u> (of **from**) (Informal, Who did he get the money from?)

1. _____ are they discussing?

   _____

2. To _____ did they deliver the flowers?

   _____

3. _____ was given the instructions?

   _____

4. _____ are they sending to fix the word processor?

   _____

5. _____ will volunteer to do this job?

   _____

Indirect Questions (Noun Clauses)

Example: a. I know <u>who</u> is watering the plants. <u>s</u> (of **is watering**)

            b. I know <u>whom</u> you want. <u>ov</u> (of **want**)

            c. I know from <u>whom</u> he got the money. <u>op</u> (of **from**)

1. We can't imagine _____ could have done such a thing.

   _____

2. They will soon announce _____ they have chosen.

   _____

3. Please let us know to _____ the money should be sent.

   _____

4. I can't remember from _____ I bought this.

   _____

5. The teachers tried to guess _____ might be appointed as the

   new principal. _____

Adjective Clauses

EXAMPLE: a. The man <u>who</u> is watering the plants is the gardener. <u>S</u> (of **is watering**)

b. The man <u>whom</u> you want is the gardener. <u>OV</u> (of **want**)

c. The man from <u>whom</u> he got the money is the gardener. <u>OP</u> (of **from**)

1. The girl with _____ she is living is a brilliant student.

   _____

2. I always appreciate a person _____ can be trusted.

   _____

3. The woman _____ we hired as a cook will start tomorrow.

   _____

4. He is a man on _____ you can depend.

   _____

5. I don't know anyone _____ can do this job.

   _____

2-5

REFLEXIVE PRONOUNS

A reflexive pronoun generally *points back to the subject*. It is used:

1. as the direct object of the verb—**You mustn't blame** *yourself* **for that mistake.**

2. as the indirect object of the verb—**I bought** *myself* **a beautiful watch.**

3. as a prepositional object:

   a. of a verb—**We should depend on** *ourselves* **rather than on others.**

   b. of an adjective—**She's angry with** *herself* **for making such a mistake.**

Supply the required reflexive pronoun.

EXAMPLE: a. Albert Schweitzer dedicated <u>himself</u> to caring for the sick in Africa. (**Himself** is the direct object of the verb **dedicated.**)

b. She made <u>herself</u> a dress. (**Herself** is the indirect object of the verb **made.**)

c. He's very selfish; he thinks only about <u>himself</u>. (**Himself** is the prepositional object of the verb **thinks**.)

d. They are ashamed of <u>themselves</u>. (**Themselves** is the prepositional object of the adjective **ashamed**.)

1. It's time I bought _____ a new car.

2. If we could only see _____ as others see us.

3. The children washed and dressed _____ quickly.[3]

4. She's quite pleased with _____ for finishing the job on time.

5. They built _____ a beautiful home.

6. Did both of you enjoy _____ at the party?

7. You should always depend on _____ rather than on someone else.

8. God helps those who help _____.

9. He's angry with _____ for misplacing the money.

10. You will all have to be responsible for _____.

11. They are always quarreling among _____.

12. He's telling a story about _____.

13. Try not to make a fool of _____.

14. They are constantly talking about _____.

15. We must now devote _____ wholeheartedly to the task at hand.

16. Their mother asked the children to behave _____.[3]

2-6
REFLEXIVE PRONOUNS AS INTENSIFIERS

Reflexive pronouns used as intensifiers are not necessary for the grammatical structure of a sentence. They merely serve to emphasize nouns or pronouns.

Intensifying a *subject*		We **ourselves** will lead the discussion. (= *we and no one else*)
	or	We will lead the discussion *ourselves*. (*Final position is possible only if the sentence or clause is short.*)
		Shakespeare **himself** could not have said it better. (= ***even Shakespeare***)
	or	Shakespeare could not have said it better **himself**.
Intensifying an *object*		I saw the chief **himself**.
		They want us to lead the discussion **ourselves**.
		We spoke to the victims **themselves**.

---

[3]The reflexive pronoun is optional in these sentences.

Use a reflexive pronoun to emphasize each of the indicated words. If the italicized word is a subject, note whether the reflexive intensifier may also appear in final position.

EXAMPLE: a.   You _yourself_ cannot believe such a thing. _yourself_

   b.   The *governor* _himself_ cannot help the condemned man. (Final position for the reflexive pronoun would cause ambiguity.)

1.   Their unexpected success at the polls surprised the *candidates*

   _____ .

2.   This package must be given to the *president* _____ .

3.   *We* _____ must do the work.

   _____

4.   *She* _____ had nothing to do with the robbery.

   _____

5.   *He* _____ told us about the matter.

   _____

6.   The report was written by *the department head* _____ .

7.   *The victims* _____ can't explain how the accident happened.

   _____

8.   *You* (plural) _____ would not care to be put into such an

   unpleasant situation. _____

9.   *The party members* _____ don't believe that their leaders

   are honest. _____

10.   *The Queen* _____ gave instructions on what to serve for the

   state dinner. _____

11.   Many people think he's a great man. *I* _____ once thought

   so _____ , but I don't any more.

12.   *He* _____ would never have permitted such a thing to hap-

   pen _____ ; someone else must have planned it.

PRONOUNS FOR GENERAL STATEMENTS

Several pronouns may be used to represent people in general (generic person).

---

we	We all get into trouble sometimes.
they (*informal*)	They grow coffee in Brazil. (*more formal*—Coffee is grown in Brazil.)
	They say that honesty is the best policy. (*more formal*—It is said that honesty is best policy.)
you (*informal*)	You have to eat in order to live.
one (*formal*)	One should do one's (*or* his *or* his or her) duty in all things.
everybody *or* **everyone**	Everybody should obey the law.

In making general statements, we should not shift from one pronoun to another.

Shift in person

> If **we** are making statements about people in general, **one** should not shift from one person to another, but **you** should be consistent in **your** use of pronouns.

Corrected to

> If **we** are making statements about people in general, **we** should not shift from one person to another, but **we** should be consistent in **our** use of pronouns.

A pronoun referring back to a noun which represents a class should have the same number (singular or plural) as the noun.

Shift in number

> The **student** must be made to understand how each lesson can be of value to **them**.

Corrected to

> The **student** must be made to understand how each lesson can be of value to **him**.[4]

---

[4](This shift in number is often made to avoid the grammatically required *him* or the awkward *him or her.* Such a choice becomes unnecessary if the plural noun *students* is used to represent the class.)

Fill in the blanks with the proper pronouns for general statements. Avoid a shift in person or number.

EXAMPLE: a. <u>One</u> should always be careful when <u>one (*or* he *or* he or she)</u> is crossing the street.
or
<u>Everybody (*or* everyone)</u> should always be careful when <u>he or she</u> is crossing the street.

b. <u>They</u> say that the number thirteen is unlucky.

c. Teachers must be sure that all of <u>their</u> students understand the point <u>they</u> are making.

d. <u>You</u> never really know what love is until <u>you</u> experience it <u>yourself</u> (reflexive).
or
<u>We</u> never really know what love is until <u>we</u> experience it <u>ourselves</u>.

1. _____ all need to relax at times.

2. _____ should be loyal to the country

_____ live in.

3. If a person practices typing every day, _____ can become an expert.

4. Doctors are responsible for the lives of _____ patients.

5. During the war everyone had to look out for _____ (reflexive).

6. _____ should not give up before

_____ absolutely have to.

7. _____ should love _____ neighbors as _____ love _____ (reflexive).

8. _____ do things somewhat differently in every country.

9. Dentists say that _____ should brush

_____ teeth every day.

10. The company expects _____ to do a full day's work.

11. _____ should not expect as much of others as

_____ expect of _____ (reflexive).

12. _____ should try to keep _____ streets clean.

2-8
PRONOUNS WITH -*EVER*

The -**ever** forms of pronouns have several uses.

Intensifiers in questions	***Whatever** made you insult that man?* ***Whoever** told you to do such a thing?*
Intensifiers in negatives (equivalent to **at all**)	*He doesn't understand any English **whatever** (or **whatsoever**). (Only these forms* *with **what** are negative intensifiers.)*
Alternatives for **no matter** **who—what—which**	***Whoever** knocks at the door, don't answer it.*
Introductory words in noun clauses	***Whoever** broke the window must pay for it.* *Take **whatever** you want. (**Whatever**=no matter what. **What** may* *also be used here.)*

Supply **whoever, whomever, whatever,** *or* **whichever.**

EXAMPLE: a. Give this to one of the boys, <u>whichever</u> one comes to the door first. (**Whichever** is used for a choice.)

b. <u>Whoever</u> gave you permission to leave the office early?

c. <u>Whatever</u> happened to those nice people who used to live next door to you?

1. He will borrow money from _____ is willing to lend it to him.

2. I have no money _____.

3. _____ finishes first will win a prize.

4. I will abide by _____ decision you make.

5. He is very grateful to _____ helps him.

6. He tells the same story to _____ he meets.

7. _____ he does is done well.

8. We'll employ _____ woman the agency sends us.

9. He'll do _____ you say.

10. _____ he paints expresses his deep spirituality.

11. _____ marries her will be a lucky man.

12. _____ TV channel he turned on, he saw nothing but game shows or soap operas.

13. We know no one _____ in this town.

14. _____ she does displeases her husband.

15. _____ is worth doing at all is worth doing well.

AGREEMENT WITH INDEFINITE PRONOUNS (1)

Each, every, either, neither require singular verbs. Pronouns referring to one of these words are singular in formal speech.

> **Each** student **is** bringing **his** (*or* **his or her**) lunch.
> (His can refer to a group of males and females together.)
> **Everyone is** expected to do **his** (*or* **his or her**) best.
> **Neither** of the girls **has** done **her** homework.

In *informal* usage, a plural verb may occur with **either, neither** but not with *each, every;* and a plural pronoun may refer to **each, every, either, neither.**

For each sentence, fill in the required form for the verb and the pronoun. Use only the present tense. Observe formal usage.

EXAMPLE: a.   Each of the boy scouts (be) <u>is</u> bringing <u>his</u> own camping equipment.

b.   All of the boy scouts (be) <u>are</u> bringing <u>their</u> own camping equipment.

1.   Everyone (have) _____   _____ own way of doing things.

2.   Each of the awards (be) _____ for a large sum of money.

3.   Either of the women (be) _____ willing to lend you

_____ car.

4.   Each employee (be) _____ being asked to contribute as

much as _____ can.

5.   Everybody in the office (seem) _____ pleased with the raise

_____ has received.

6.   Neither of the lamps (be) _____ suitable for this table.

7.   Both of the lamps (be) _____ suitable for this table.

8.   Each student (be) _____ requested to ask

_____ parents to come to the parent teacher association meeting.

9.   Either you or I (be) _____ mistaken.[5]

10.   Every apartment in the building (need) _____ some repairs.

[5]In formal usage, the verb agrees with the noun or pronoun after **(n)or.**

2-10

AGREEMENT WITH INDEFINITE PRONOUNS (2)

A pronoun of indefinite quantity like **some, all, none, most** plus an **of** phrase requires a verb that agrees with the *noun in the* **of** *phrase*.

> Some of the **machines need** to be repaired.
>
> Some of the **machinery needs** to be repaired.

The same rule applies if words that refer to a part (**half, rest, remainder**) *or* a fraction (**one-third, three-fourths**) are used.

> Half of the **pie was** eaten.
>
> Half of the **pies were** eaten.

Use the required form of the verb **be**.

EXAMPLE: a.   All of her jewelry (*past*) <u>was</u> put in a safety vault.

           b.   All of her jewels (*past*) <u>were</u> put in a safety vault.

1.   None of the pies (*past*) _____ eaten.[6]

2.   None of the dessert (*past*) _____ eaten.

3.   All of the information on the report (*present*) _____ correct.

4.   All of the statistics on the report (*present*) _____ correct.

5.   Most of his luggage (*past*) _____ lost on his last trip.

6.   Most of his bags (*past*) _____ lost on his last trip.

7.   Some of that poet's work (*present*) _____ very fine.

8.   Some of that poet's works (*present*) _____ very fine.

9.   Most of the merchandise (*present perfect*) _____ sold.

10.   Most of the goods (*present perfect*) _____ sold.

11.   All of this fruit (*present*) _____ from their garden.

12.   All of these apples (*present*) _____ from their garden.

13.   Half of the turkey (*present*) _____ for today's dinner.

14.   Half of the dinner guests (*past*) _____ staying with their

     hosts overnight. The remainder (*past*) _____ taking the last train back to town.

15.   Almost one-third of the people in the world (*present*) _____ always hungry.

---

[6]Some conservative handbooks claim that only a singular verb should be used with **none**.

Other, another are pronouns used mainly in adjective function.

Other	
with a plural noun (most common use)	*This pen doesn't work. Try one of the **other** ones.*
with a singular noun (only if a determiner like **the, any, some, each** precedes it)	*This pen doesn't work. The **other** pen doesn't, either.*
Another	
only with a singular noun	*Please give me **another** (= a different) pen. This one doesn't work.*
	*Would you like **another** (= an additional) piece of pie?*

Since **another** consists of **an** + **other**, no other determiner can precede it.
Other, another may also function as nouns, with the word **one** understood.

He has two sisters. One is going to college, the **other** is working as a secretary.

One person may enjoy living in a big city, while **another** may prefer living in a small town.

Others is the plural of **other** in noun function only.

Some people like to watch TV at night, while **others** (= other people) prefer to read a good book.

Some of the search party went to the right, the **others** (= the rest) went to the left.

Use other, another, or others.

Example: a. This route to Boston takes too long. There must be <u>another</u> way that is shorter.

b. He held a book in one hand and his notes in the <u>other</u>.

1. He has always liked to travel to _____ countries.

2. Some plants grow well in this climate. _____, however, cannot be grown here.

3. _____ accident occurred in the same spot where one occurred last week.

4. I'll have to use the duplicate key. I lost the _____ one.

5. Any _____ person than her husband would have lost patience with her.

6. We didn't put quite enough plates on the table. Please hand me

    _____ one.

7. He had a bad quarrel with his friend last week. Now they're not talking to each

    _____.

8. Here are two books. One is for Mary, the _____ is for Jack.

9. One person may like to spend his vacation at the seashore;

    _____ may choose to go to the mountains.

10. Their house is not very large. They plan to add _____ room to it.

11. I listen only to this radio station. The _____ don't give the news.

12. Some _____ people might not persevere, but he is determined to get to the top of that mountain.

13. A political system that works well in one country may not work so well in

    _____ country.

2-12
EXPLETIVE *THERE* vs. EXPLETIVE *IT*

The expletives **it** and **there** fill subject position but have no meaning of their own. Expletive **there** commonly occurs in the following types of sentences.

1. **There** + **be** + (pro)noun + *expression of place*

    > There's nobody **here.**
    > There's a piano **in the room.**

2. **There** + **be** + noun with *adjective modifiers*

    > There was once **a very wicked** king.
    > There are **three** reasons **for rejecting that proposal.**

3. **There** + **be** + noun + *-ing participle*

    > There is a sale **going on** at the bookstore. (= A sale is going on at the bookstore.)

There is a strong wind **coming up** from the west. (= A strong wind is coming up from the west.)

In a sentence with expletive **there**, the verb agrees with the actual subject that follows it.

There **is** a **book** on the desk.
There **are** some **books** on the desk.

Expletive **it** is often found in the following constructions.

1. **It** + **be** + adjective + *adverbial construction*

    It's gloomy **here.**
    It's pleasant **in the garden.**
    It would be wise **if you went there now.**

2. **It** + **be** + an expression of:

identification	Who is it? It's the *repairman.*
weather	It's *cold* outside.
time	It's *Wednesday* (*or ten o'clock, or January 25*).
distance	It is *five miles from the library to my house.*

Only a singular verb is used with expletive **it.**

Supply it is, there is, there are.

EXAMPLE: a.   <u>It is</u> raining outside now.

　　　　　　 b.   <u>There is</u> no place like home.

　　　　　　 c.   <u>There are</u> many simple recipes in this cookbook.

1. _____ more comfortable over here.

2. _____ someone waiting in the office to see you.

3. Who is at the door? _____ Mary.

4. _____ two good reasons why you shouldn't go there.

5. _____ not a house to be seen for miles around.

6. _____ very warm today.

7. _____ many books on man-made satellites in the library.

8. _____ too cold to go outside.

9. What time _____? _____ a quarter past two.

10. _____ a lot of changes that should be made.

11. _____ more efficient if you do it this way.

12. _____ snowing very hard now.

13. _____ more births than deaths in some countries.

14. _____ many ways of telling a lie.

15. _____ only one way of telling the truth.

16. _____ often very windy near the ocean.

17. _____ some people who are never satisfied.

18. _____ no fool like an old fool.

19. _____ so hot that we can't work.

20. _____ something wrong with this typewriter.

21. _____ enough books for everyone in the class.

22. _____ too noisy here for us to study.

23. _____ too much noise here for us to study.

24. _____ a few pages missing from today's newspaper.

2-13
ANTICIPATORY *IT*

An anticipatory **it** construction is used to avoid having a long noun structure appear in subject position. The construction without anticipatory **it** is felt as more formal.

When anticipatory **it** appears in subject position, the actual noun structure subject is found at the end of the sentence, after the predicate.

Infinitive phrase subject	*To become a good doctor requires much training and experience.*
with anticipatory **it** (less formal)	*It requires much training and experience to become a good doctor.*
That clause subject	*That he was able to sell that old car of his was a surprise to us.*
with anticipatory **it** (less formal)	*It was a surprise to us that he was able to sell that old car of his.*

Change each sentence so that it begins with **it**.

IT with Infinitive Phrase Subject

EXAMPLE: a. To take a drive in the country is very pleasant.

It is very pleasant to take a drive in the country.

b. For me to do that is quite difficult.
   It is quite difficult for me to do that.

1. To fill out all these forms is very time-consuming.

_____

2. To do some exercise every day is good for one's health.

_____

3. For man to land a spaceship on the moon is now possible.

_____

4. For her to work so hard makes no sense.

_____

5. To speak English well is difficult for foreign students.

_____

_____

IT with THAT Noun Clause Subject

EXAMPLE: That he should resent such a remark is natural.
   It is natural that he should resent such a remark.

1. That she is very talented is quite evident.

_____

2. That we will never finish on time is becoming apparent.

_____

3. That he failed his examinations is a shame.

_____

4. That he might be very ill never occurred to me.

_____

5. That she couldn't have her way frustrated her.

_____

REVIEW OF PRONOUNS

A. Supply the correct form of the pronoun.

1. Every nation has (it) _____ own special problems.

2. Can you tell me which house is (they) _____?

3. (Who) _____ money was used to finance the deal?

4. He is a good friend (I) _____. (two words)

5. Some students (her) _____ were on a TV discussion program. (two words)

6. That car (they) _____ always gave them trouble. (two words)

7. If we could only see (we) _____ as others see us.

8. Did both of you enjoy (you) _____ at the party?

9. God helps those who help (them) _____.

10. They are always quarreling among (they) _____.

11. He didn't bring a coat, so I lent him (I) _____.

12. (Who) _____ was given the instructions?

13. Between (you) _____ and (I)
_____, she's not very happy in her new home.

14. They will soon announce (who) _____ they have chosen.

15. I can't remember from (who) _____ I bought this.

B. Supply the required pronoun.

1. The teachers tried to guess _____ might be appointed as the new principal.

2. The girl with _____ Mary is living is a brilliant student.

3. He is a man on _____ you can depend.

4. If a person practices typing every day, _____ can become an expert.

5. Doctors are responsible for the lives of _____ patients.

6. He will borrow money from _____ is willing to lend it to him.

7. I will abide by _____ decision you make.

8. He is very grateful to _____ helps him.

9. _____ he does is done well.

10. _____ marries her will be a lucky man.

C. Supply the correct form of the verb. Use the present tense unless a time word requires the past.

1. Each of the awards (be) _____ for a large sum of money.

2. Every apartment in the building (need) _____ some repairs.

3. Most of his luggage (be) _____ lost on his last trip.

4. Some of that poet's works (be) _____ very fine.

5. All of the information on the report (be) _____ correct.

6. Everyone (have) _____ his own way of doing things.

7. Each of the awards (be) _____ for a large sum of money.

8. All of the statistics in the report _____ correct.

9. All of the scenery in this part of the country (be) _____ interesting.

10. Most of their furniture (be) _____ very old.

D. Rewrite these sentences, beginning with *it* or *there.*

1. To get up early in the morning is difficult.

_____

2. Someone in the office is waiting to see you.

_____

3. That he was able to sell that old car of his was a surprise to us.

_____

4. To become a good doctor requires much training and experience.

_____

5. Many good books on man-made satellites are in the library.

_____

6. For him to work so hard makes no sense.

_____

7. A storm is approaching.

_____

8. That we will never finish on time is becoming apparent.

_____

9. Several aspects of this subject require further discussion.

_____

10. Plenty of towels are in the bathroom.

_____

STRUCTURAL DESCRIPTION OF VERBS

Function	The verb is the grammatical "center" of the sentence.
Position	The verb appears after the subject and before any type of complement in the predicate. (See position of nouns.)
Form	The verb has three regular inflectional endings—*-s, -ed, -ing*. Auxiliaries are also used with verbs to form *verb phrases*. The one-part verbs and the verb phrases that may function as verbs in the predicate are:

	Active Voice	Progressive		**Passive Voice**	Progressive
Tense					
Present	offer*, offers*	am / is / are } offering		am / is / are } offered	am / is / are } being offered
Past	offered*	was / were } offering		was / were } offered	was / were } being offered
Future	will / shall } offer	will / shall } be offering		will / shall } be offered	
Present perfect	have / has } offered	have / has } been offering		have / has } been offered	
Past perfect	had offered	had been offering		had been offered	
Future perfect	will / shall } have offered	will / shall } have been offering		will / shall } have been offered	

*These auxiliary-less verbs are called the *simple* present and the *simple* past.

The auxiliaries **can–could, may–might, must, would, should** also help to form the verb in the predicate. The forms of verb phrases used with these auxiliaries are:

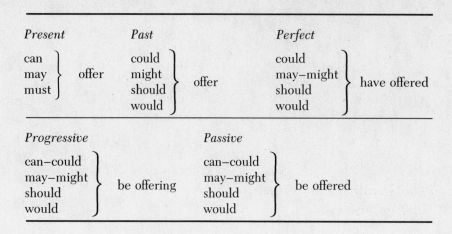

Present		*Past*		*Perfect*	
can may must	} offer	could might should would	} offer	could may–might should would	} have offered

Progressive		*Passive*	
can–could may–might should would	} be offering	can–could may–might should would	} be offered

3-1
ADDING INFLECTIONAL ENDINGS

Add **-s** (third person singular) **-ed** (past tense), and **-ing** (present participle) to the following verbs.

	-s	*-ed*	*-ing*

Verbs with Final -y or -ie

study	studies	studied	studying
marry			
hurry			
qualify			
carry			
worry			
play	plays	played	playing
employ			
convey			
enjoy			
display			
die	dies	died	(*irreg.*) **dying**
tie			(*irreg.*)
lie (*recline*)		(*irreg.*)	(*irreg.*)
lie (*tell an untruth*)			

Verbs with Final -e

advise	advises	advised	advising
change			
dine			

	-s	-ed	-ing
continue			
write		*(irreg.)*	
argue			
shine		*(irreg.)*	
lose		*(irreg.)*	
agree	**agrees**	**agreed**	**agreeing**
guarantee			
free			
see		*(irreg.)*	

Verbs with Final Single Consonants Preceded by Single Vowels

	-s	-ed	-ing
plán	**pláns**	**plánned**	**plánning**
dróp			
whíp			
bég			
control	**contróls**	**contrólled**	**contrólling**
permít			
occúr			
prefér			
regrét			
equíp			
trável	**trávels**	**tráveled** (*U.S.*)	**tráveling** (*U.S.*)
		trávelled (*Brit.*)	**trávelling** (*Brit.*)
wórship			
cáncel			
équal			
tótal			
bénefit	**bénefits**	**bénefited**	**bénefiting**
intérpret			
devélop			

Verbs with Final Sibilants (Spelled -s, -z, -ch, -sh, -x)

	-s	-ed	-ing
push	**pushes**	**pushed**	**pushing**
guess			
quiz			
watch			
teach		*(irreg.)*	
ambush			
fix			
buzz			
crush			

3-2
DERIVATION (1)
ADDING THE SUFFIXES *-EN*, *-IZE*, *-IFY*

Change the following nouns to verbs by adding the suffixes **-en, -ize, -ify**. Make whatever changes are necessary.

apology _____

fright _____

character _____

beauty _____

author _____

haste _____

critic _____

class _____

emphasis _____

liquid _____

length _____

drama _____

memory _____

satire _____

strength _____

standard _____

terror _____

threat _____

sympathy _____

colony _____

glory _____

summary _____

symbol _____

height _____

3-3
DERIVATION (2)
ADDING PREFIXES *EN-*, *BE-*, *AC-*, *IM-*

Change the following nouns to verbs by adding the prefixes **en-, be-, ac-, im-**.

custom _____

friend _____

joy _____

head _____

circle _____

climate _____

force _____

knowledge _____

slave _____

prison _____

title _____

witch _____

trust _____

courage _____

3-4
DERIVATION (3)
CHANGING NOUNS TO VERBS

In the blank spaces supply the verbs that are related to the italicized nouns. Use the correct verb forms.

1. The *production* of coal in our country is very great. How much coal does your country

   _____?

2. It is so easy to see through his *pretenses*. Why must he always

   _____ to be more important than he is?

3. The *applause* was deafening. There was no one in the room who was not

   _____ loudly.

4. If he won't take my *advice*, why did he ask me to _____ him?

5. His ultimate *success* depends on how well he _____ in every step along the way.

6. The *explosion* was heard for miles around. No one knew what had caused the airplane

   to _____.

7. It's time for the baby's *bath*. Would you like to _____ him?

8. The *loss* of life was very great in the last war. In the next war we may

   _____ many more men than we

   _____ in the previous war.

9. I'm all out of *breath*. It's difficult to _____ in this high altitude.

10. His *choice* of words was unfortunate. Sometimes it's important to

    _____ the right words. In his place, I would have

    _____ words that were not so emotional.

11. Nostradamus made many *prophecies*. He _____ that the world would be destroyed in the year 2000.

12. The kind of *proof* you have offered does not _____ conclusively that you are right.

13. He may _____ other people, but I can see right through his *deception*.

14. He irritates everyone by his *insults*. Can't he be with people without

    _____ them?[1]

[1]Some nouns and verbs have the same form—an answer, to answer; a surprise, to surprise; an escape, to escape. Other nouns differ from verbs only by the shift in stress—a pérmit, to permít; some prógress, to progréss; a récord, to recórd.

The tense forms of a number of verbs differ from the regular forms. The principal parts of such verbs must be known before the proper tense forms can be used. The first principal part of a verb is the *simple form of the verb* (the infinitive without **to**), the second principal part is the *past tense*, the third principal part is the *past participle* (used for the perfect tenses or for the passive forms). Thus, the principal parts for the regular verb **offer** are—**offer, offered, offered.**

The exercises that follow are grouped according to the kind of irregularity the verbs show.[2] Supply the proper verb forms for the past tense; then change each sentence to the present perfect, using an appropriate time expression for this tense (**just, already, so far, up to now, always, never, sometimes, this morning,** etc.)

All Three Principal Parts Are Different

sing, sang, sung   **begin, drink, ring, shrink** (past also **shrunk**),
                                sing, sink (past tense also **sunk**), **swim**

EXAMPLE: I (begin) <u>began</u> the work yesterday.
             <u>I have already begun the work.</u>

1. They (drink) _____ too much beer yesterday.

       _____

2. The bell (ring) _____ a few minutes ago.

       _____

3. We (sing) _____ Christmas carols last night.

       _____

4. The ship (sink) _____ some time ago.

       _____

           break, broke, broken   **break, choose, freeze, steal, speak, weave**

5. Our club (choose) _____ a new president last month.

       _____

6. The bank robber (steal) _____ the money the day before yesterday.

       _____

---

[2]A list of irregular verbs is given in the appendix in alphabetical order.

7. They (freeze) _____ the food before they shipped it.

_____

drive, drove, driven   **drive, ride,[3] (a)rise, write[3]**

8. He (drive) _____ too fast last night.

_____

9. She (ride) _____ a beautiful white horse when she was young.

_____

10. We (write) _____ the letter yesterday.

_____

11. The sun (rise) _____ at six this morning.

_____

In the following exercises, the time words for the two tenses have been omitted, but keep in mind that the past tense represents *definite* past (**yesterday, last year, a week ago**), while the present perfect represents *indefinite* past that is related to the present (with **since, for, so far,** etc.)

blow, blew, blown   **blow, draw, fly, grow, know, throw, withdraw**

EXAMPLE: The artist (draw) <u>drew; has drawn</u> the picture.

12. The boys (throw) _____ pennies into the well.

13. The helicopter (fly) _____ over the city.

14. The boy (grow) _____ very fast.

wear, wore, worn   **bear** (*past participle* **borne** and **born**)[4] **swear, tear, wear**

15. He (swear) _____ to get revenge.

16. She (bear) _____ her troubles without complaint.

17. His wife (wear) _____ her new gown to the ball.

bite, bit, bitten   **bite** (*also* **bit, bit**), **chide** (*also* **chided, chided**), **hide** (*also* **hid, hid**)

18. The dog (bite) _____ the boy.

[3]In these words, the *d* and the *t* are doubled for the past participle.
[4]**Borne** is the usual past participle of **bear** in all uses except with **be**. **Be born** represents the fact of birth—**She was born in France.**

19. He (hide) _____ the money under the bed.

shake, shook, shaken   forsake, mistake, shake, take

20. He (forsake) _____ his wife for another woman.

21. I (mistake) _____ you for an acquaintance.

22. They (take) _____ the wrong train.

Other Verbs Whose Principal Parts Are All Different

be	was	been
do	did	done
eat	ate	eaten
fall	fell	fallen
go	went	gone
lie	lay	lain
see	saw	seen
(a)wake	(a)woke	(a)waked, *British* (a)woke *or* (a)woken
	sometimes (a)waked	

23. He (do) _____ the work very efficiently.

24. She (eat) _____ her dinner too fast.

25. The girl (fall) _____ on the ice.

26. They (go) _____ to the park.

27. He (lie) _____ in bed all day.

28. I (see) _____ a good movie.

29. They (be) _____ in the country for three weeks.

30. We (awake) _____ in time to see the sun rise.

3-6
IRREGULAR VERBS (2)

Supply the verb forms for the past tense and the present perfect tense.

Second and Third Principal Parts Are Alike

hang, hung   cling, dig, hang,[5] sling, slink, spin, stick, sting, strike,[6] string, swing, wring

[5]When **hang** refers to death by suspension by the neck, the past tense as well as the past participle is **hanged**.

[6]**Stricken** is the past participle of **strike** when used figuratively as an adjective—conscience-stricken, terror-stricken, stricken with a disease.

EXAMPLE: A bee (sting) <u>stung</u>; <u>has stung</u> him in the arm.

1. She (hang) _____ the clothes on the line.

2. They (dig) _____ a hole for the tree.

3. He (stick) _____ the notice on the bulletin board.

4. The pendulum (swing) _____ back and forth.

feed, fed	bleed, breed, feed, flee, lead, speed
or	
creep, crept	creep, dream,[7] feel, keep, kneel,[7] leap,[7] leave, mean, meet, sleep, sweep, weep

5. He (mean) _____ what he said.

6. The snake (creep) _____ along the ground.

7. He (feed) _____ his dog twice a day.

8. The refugees (flee) _____ from their pursuers.

9. He (keep) _____ his money in the safe.

10. The captain (lead) _____ the men.

11. She (meet) _____ many interesting people at that party.

12. She (sweep) _____ the dirt under the rug.

bring, brought	beseech, bring, buy, catch, fight, seek, teach, think

13. We (think) _____ about these problems for a long time.

14. The boy (catch) _____ a cold.

15. They (fight) _____ a losing battle.

16. The secretary (bring) _____ her lunch with her.

17. Her mother (teach) _____ her how to sew.

bend, bent	bend, lend, rend, send, spend

18. He (spend) _____ too much money for that car.

19. She (lend) _____ her neighbor her vacuum cleaner.

20. The strong wind (bend) _____ the tree.

bind, bound	bind, find, grind, wind

21. The butcher (grind) _____ the meat.

22. I (find) _____ a watch in the street.

[7]These verbs also have the regular alternatives **dreamed, kneeled, leaped.**

23. The doctor (bind) _____ the wound with a clean bandage.

pay, paid   **lay, mislay, pay, say**

24. He (mislay) _____ the report.

25. They (pay) _____ all their bills.

sell, sold   **sell, tell**

26. They (sell) _____ their car.

Other Verbs Whose Second and Third Principal Parts Are Alike

abide (*literary*)	abode
build	built
clothe	clad (*literary*) (*also* **clothed**)
forget	forgot (*or, past participle* **forgotten**, *American usage*)
get	got (*or, past participle* **gotten**, *American usage*)
have	had
hear	heard
hold	held
behold (*literary*)	beheld
withhold	withheld
light	lit[8]
lose	lost
make	made
shine	shone[9]
shoe	shod
shoot	shot
sit	sat
slide	slid
stand	stood
understand	understood
withstand	withstood
tread (*literary*)	trod (*or, past participle* **trodden**)
win	won

27. I (hear) _____ the news on the radio.

28. He (hold) _____ many important positions.

29. The policeman (shoot) _____ the robber.

30. I (forget) _____ to mail the letter.

---

[8]Also, **lighted**, meaning *to provide light,* or as an adjective (**A well-lighted room**).
[9]**Shined** is used for the transitive verb—**The boy shined his shoes.**

31. He (lose) _____ money in the stock market.

32. The men (withstand) _____ the fierce attack by the enemy.

33. He (win) _____ some money at the horse races.

34. The sun (shine) _____ very brightly.

All Three Principal Parts Are Alike

bet (sometimes **betted** for the past tense and the past participle)

bid (meaning *offer money at an auction*)

broadcast (sometimes **broadcasted** for the *past tense* and the *past participle*)

burst

cast

cost

hit

hurt

knit (*also* **knitted** for the *past tense* and the *past participle*)

let

put

read

rid

set

shed

shut

slit

spit (sometimes **spat** for the *past tense* and the *past participle*)

split

spread

thrust

35. The boy (hit) _____ the dog.

36. The radio (broadcast) _____ the President's entire speech.

37. He (shut) _____ the door.

38. The pipes (burst) _____ because of the cold.

39. His carelessness (cost) _____ him his life.

40. He (spread) _____ the butter on the bread.

First and Third Principal Parts Are Alike

come	came	come
become	became	become
overcome	overcame	overcome
run	ran	run

41. He (overcome) _____ all difficulties.

42. The children (run) _____ away.

First and Second Principal Parts Are Alike

beat   beat   beaten (*or* **beat**)

43. He (beat) _____ the dog with a stick.

Use the **past tense** (second principal part), or the **past participle** (third principal part) of the irregular verbs in parentheses.

EXAMPLE: a.   Many planes (fly) <u>flew</u> over this village a few minutes ago. (past tense)

   b.   She has (wear) <u>worn</u> her new dress only once. (past participle after the auxiliary **have**)

   c.   The window was (break) <u>broken</u> some time ago. (past participle after the auxiliary **be** with a passive verb)

1.   I fell asleep just as soon as I (lie) _____ down on the bed.

2.   No one knows where the robbers have (hide) _____ the money.

3.   The girl (fall) _____ off the horse yesterday and (hurt) _____ herself badly.

4.   I have (see) _____ several good movies this year.

5.   The clothes were (hang) _____ on the line to dry.

6.   It was (think) _____ that he had met with an accident.

7.   The money was (lend) _____ to him by a friend.

8.   All the bills were (pay) _____ yesterday.

9.   The apartment house was (build) _____ ten years ago.

10.   Our team (win) _____ the game yesterday.

11.   The same car (cost) _____ $500 less a year ago.

12.   She doesn't remember where she (lay) _____ the packages yesterday.

13.   Construction on the building was (begin) _____ three years ago.

14.   He didn't get up until long after the sun had (rise) _____.

15.   The picture was (draw) _____ by a famous artist.

16.   He (swim) _____ so far out from shore that the lifeguard signaled for him to come back.

17.   A hole has already been (dig) _____ for the well.

18.   He was (strike) _____ in the face by a baseball.

19.   What is (mean) _____ by this word?

20.   She has (bring) _____ two of her children with her.

21.   We seem to have (lose) _____ our way.

22.   The money was (put) _____ in the bank right away.

23.   He has (lie) _____ in bed all day.

24. He was (choose) _____ to lead the men.

25. He has (drive) _____ many racing cars.

26. Her coat was (tear) _____ on a nail.

27. The boy was (bite) _____ by a mosquito.

28. Several notes were (stick) _____ up on the wall.

29. This tray was (buy) _____ at Woolworth's.

30. The holdup victim was (shoot) _____ in the arm.

31. He has already (sleep) _____ for ten hours.

32. The suspected thief is being (seek) _____ by the police.

33. She has always (dream) _____ of being a ballerina.

34. The watch has already been (wind) _____ today.

35. She (weave) _____ the rug on her own loom.

36. The child (cling) _____ fearfully to her mother.

37. She (weep) _____ with joy when she heard that her daughter had passed the bar exam.

38. The announcement was (read) _____ to all the members.

39. The robber (bind) _____ his victim to a tree.

40. The dictator is such a tyrant that many people have (flee)

_____ from the country.

3-8
SIMPLE PRESENT TENSE
vs. PRESENT PROGRESSIVE TENSE

Simple Present	Present Progressive
1. expresses *repeated action* (includes the past, present, and future) **The earth revolves around the sun.** (general truth) **I go there very often.** (custom)	1. expresses *one action in the present* 　a. of short duration 　　**He's studying the lesson.** 　　**He's writing a letter.** 　b. of long duration 　　**He's studying English.** 　　**He's writing a book.**
2. expresses *non-action* (state or condition) **He seems tired.** **She loves her children.** **I remember him.** **I hear some music.** (vs. **I am listening to some music.**) **The rose smells sweet.** (vs. **She's smelling the rose.**)	2. expresses *the beginning, progression or end of an action* **It is beginning to snow.** **My cold is becoming worse.**

3. expresses *future action* (especially with verbs of arriving and departing—usually requires a future time word)

We leave tomorrow.
The ship sails next week.

3. expresses *future action* (often requires a future time word)

He's giving a lecture tomorrow.
The ship is sailing next week.

Supply the simple present or the present progressive form of the verb. In a few sentences either form may be used.

EXAMPLE: a. The milk (taste) <u>tastes</u> sour. (The simple present is used with verbs of the senses—**feel, taste, smell**.

   b. She (taste) <u>is tasting</u> the soup to see if it needs more salt.

   c. The wind (blow) <u>is blowing</u> very hard outside.

1. We must stop talking. The play (begin) _____ now.

2. She (try)[10] _____ to finish her work early today.

3. The weather (get) _____ colder and colder these days.

4. I (hope) _____ to see you again.

5. We (plan) _____ to buy a house soon.

6. We (go) _____ to the movies tonight.

7. The sun (rise) _____ in the east and (set)

    _____ in the west.

8. I sometimes (forget) _____ to take my keys when I (leave)

    _____ the house.

9. She (take) _____ a nap every afternoon.

10. Listen! I (hear) _____ some loud noises outside.

11. He (listen) _____ to the radio at the moment.

12. I (look) _____ out the window right now. I (see)

    _____ some children in the street.

13. Right now I (watch) _____ the children play outside.

14. We (understand) _____ now why he was so angry.

15. He (admire) _____ his father very much.

16. He (say) _____ he can do it for you.[11]

17. She (consider) _____ entering the university.

18. He (write) _____ a book on Africa.

[10]The verb **try** is often used in the progressive forms if the sentence refers to one action.
[11]The simple present is often used for verbs of saying and telling.

19. What (you think) _____ about?

20. What (you think) _____ of the new plan?

21. All the students (have) _____ a good time at the party.

22. At present he (live) _____ in California.

23. You (waste) _____ your time doing it that way.

24. Many people (enjoy) _____ going to the beach.

25. He (spend) _____ this week at the beach; he (enjoy)

    _____ himself very much.

26. Americans (celebrate) _____ Independence Day on July 4.

27. She always (interfere) _____ in other people's affairs.[12]

28. She (spend) _____ too much money on clothes.

29. He (stay) _____ at a very luxurious hotel.

30. Water (boil) _____ at 212 degrees Fahrenheit and (freeze)

    _____ at 32 degrees.

31. They (be) _____ at the station now. They (wait)

    _____ for their train to arrive.

3-9
SIMPLE PAST TENSE
vs. PAST PROGRESSIVE TENSE

Both forms of the past tense represent *definite past*. They refer to events that were completed before the statement is made. They are often accompanied by such expressions of definite past as **yesterday, last year, two weeks ago.**

The past progressive emphasizes *duration of an action* in the past—**What were you doing all day yesterday?** The past action may be of short duration, perhaps one point in the past—**What were you doing at ten o'clock last night?**

Use the simple or progressive form for the past tense. In some sentences both past tense forms are possible.

EXAMPLE: a. Just as he (reach) <u>reached</u> the bus stop, the bus (pass) <u>passed</u> by him.

b. He (work) <u>was working</u> in a restaurant the last time I (see) <u>saw</u> him.

1. The minute we (receive) _____ his gift, we (write)

    _____ him a note of thanks.

[12]With **always, constantly, perpetually,** the progressive form of the verb may also be used.

2. When they (hear) _____ the burglar alarm go off, they (call)

   _____ the police.

3. They (eat) _____ dinner in the cafeteria a few minutes ago.

4. At 7 o'clock last night I (eat) _____ dinner.

5. Everyone (enjoy) _____ himself at the party.

6. Shakespeare (write) _____ his great plays many years ago.

7. All last year he (prepare) _____ for the bar examination.

8. After the movie (be) _____ over, they (go)

   _____ to the restaurant for coffee.

9. Where is the dog? I (see) _____ him only a few minutes ago.

10. As soon as he (open) _____ the door, his son (run over)

    _____ to greet him.

11. The guards quickly (catch) _____ the prisoner who (try)

    _____ to escape.

12. She (cut) _____ her finger while she (prepare)

    _____ dinner.

13. When the teacher (walk) _____ into the classroom, the stu-

    dents (become) _____ quiet.

14. They (leave) _____ town some time last month.

15. We reached the lake just as the sun (set)[13] _____.

16. In Columbus' day, people (believe) _____ that the earth (be)

    _____ flat.

3-10
PAST PROGRESSIVE TENSE

Wherever possible, change the verbs to progressive forms. Keep in mind that the progressive emphasizes *duration of a single event.*

EXAMPLE: a. What did he think about my plan?
           (*no change possible*)

           b. She thought about the accident all night long.
           She was thinking about the accident all night long.

---

[13]In some sentences, the simple past refers to completed action; the past progressive refers to action that is still going on.

    c. The driver stopped the bus very quickly.
      (*no change possible*)

1. We watched television last night.

   _____

2. They opened the new store last week.

   _____

3. The telephone rang all day long.

   _____

4. He got to the platform just as the train left.

   _____

5. He counted his change several times before he left the store.

   _____

   _____

6. At the party last night, people sang, danced, and ate.

   _____

   _____

7. The children played in the snow all afternoon long.

   _____

   _____

8. The typist omitted a few words from the letter.

   _____

9. She held on to the child very tightly.

   _____

10. They argued all evening long about who would win the election.

    _____

    _____

11. It rained very hard last night.

    _____

12. They sat so close to the stage that they could observe every gesture of the performers.

    _____

    _____

PAST PROGRESSIVE WITH TIME CLAUSES

One continuous past action may be interrupted by a non-continuous past action.

She was washing the dishes when the phone rang.

The past progressive form is used for the continuous action.

A. Combine each set of sentences so that the *second sentence* becomes a when clause. Use the required verb forms. Do not use a comma before the time expression at the end of the sentence.

EXAMPLE: I (cross) the street.
            I (see) an accident.

   <u>I was crossing the street when I saw an accident.</u>

1. She (do) her homework.
    She (become) very sleepy.

    _____

2. The refugees (walk) along the road.
    Some planes (appear) overhead.

    _____

3. She (prepare) dinner.
    A quarrel (break out) among the children.

    _____

4. They (eat) breakfast.
    They (hear) someone knock at the door.

    _____

5. She (put) some water in the coffee pot.
    She (notice) a leak in the pot.

    _____

6. The old gentleman (walk) in the park.
    A man with a gun (approach) him.

    _____

7. They (watch) television.
    The lights (go out).

    _____

8. The student next to me (daydream) in class.
    The teacher (address) a question to him.

    _____

9. The children (play) in the street.
    A stranger (walk) over to them.

    _____

10. The family (eat) dinner.
    The telephone (ring).

    _____

11. The hero (embrace) the heroine.
    Someone in the theater (shout) "Fire."

    _____

12. The orchestra members (get) ready to start the performance.
    They (hear) some commotion in the rear of the concert hall.

    _____

B. Many of the sentences of the form **I was doing something when something happened** may also take the form **While I was doing something, something happened.**

> She **was washing** the dishes when the phone **rang.**
>
> or While she **was washing** the dishes, the phone **rang.** (A comma is often used
>   after a long time expression at the beginning of a sentence.)

Note that no matter which statement becomes the time clause, past progressive form is used for the continuous action.

As or **just as** may be alternatives for **while** in this kind of time clause.

> Just as we **were sitting** down to dinner, the phone **rang.**

Combine the sets of sentences in A so that the *first sentence* becomes a **while** or **(just) as** clause.

EXAMPLE: While I was crossing the street, I saw an accident.

3-12
FUTURE TIME

There are several ways to express future time.

future tense	auxiliary **will**—may be used for all persons auxiliary **shall**—used for the first person (considered formal usage in the United States) progressive future—used for a *single action* especially if it has duration
simple present tense	especially with verbs of arriving and departing—requires a future time expression **(later, next week, tomorrow)**
present progressive tense	used with many verbs expressing action (often requires a future time expression)
be going to	often adds the idea of *intention* or *expectation* to future time

For the following sentences, add the other ways of expressing future time.

EXAMPLE: a. The ship will sail tomorrow.

    The ship will be sailing tomorrow. (future progressive)

    The ship sails tomorrow. (simple present)

    The ship is sailing tomorrow. (present progressive)

    The ship is going to sail tomorrow. (**be going to**)

   b. He will call you tomorrow.

    He will be calling you tomorrow. (future progressive)

    He is going to call you tomorrow. (**be going to**)

1. I will meet him later.

_____

_____

_____

_____

2. We will give a party tomorrow.

_____

_____

_____

_____

3. She will bake some cookies tonight.

_____

_____

_____

_____

4. They will return next week.

_____

_____

_____

_____

5. The travel agency will plan our itinerary.

_____

_____

_____

_____

6. The plane will arrive at 10:00 o'clock.

_____

_____

_____

7. They will write us from London in a few days.

_____

_____

_____

_____

3-13
FUTURE PROGRESSIVE TENSE

Wherever possible, change the verbs to progressive form. Keep in mind that the future progressive form, like the present progressive, may refer to a single action that has very short duration.

1. We shall arrive tomorrow.

_____

2. He will get a raise in salary soon.

_____

3. I will telephone him later tonight.

_____

4. He will be angry if you don't come.

_____

5. They will buy a house next year.

_____

6. My aunt will visit me soon.

_____

7. He will finish his book this year.

_____

8. You will never forget that trip.

_____

9. Our club meets next week.

_____

10. You will love her the moment you meet her.

_____

3-14
PRESENT PERFECT TENSE

The present perfect tense represents time that begins in the past and extends to the present, either in actual fact or in the mind of the speaker. It is not used with definite time words like *yesterday, last year*.

The kinds of time words that express past-to-present time are:

since *or* **for**	I have lived here for **six** years. (period of time ending in the present—**for** may be omitted) *or* I have lived here since 1980. (beginning of past-to-present time)
so far, up to now, up to the present	We have had no trouble with our television set so far (*or* up to now).
frequency words—**always, never, ever, often, sometimes, occasionally,** etc. (indefinite past-to-present time)	He has always lived in this town. This is the best book I have ever read.
just, already (negative **yet**), **finally**	Our dinner guests have just arrived.
recently, lately[14] (time very close to the present)	She has not seen him recently.

If no time word is given, either the past or the present perfect tense is possible, depending on whether the time is felt as definite past, or past to present.

Supply the correct forms of the present perfect tense. For this exercise, do not use the progressive forms. Note the expressions that call for the use of the present perfect tense.

EXAMPLE: a. Ruth (just return) <u>has just returned</u> from South America.

   b. We (already have) <u>have already had</u> breakfast.

1. The professor (lecture) _____ for over an hour.

2. They (know) _____ each other since childhood.

---

[14]Informally, except for **since, for,** the past tense is often used with these time words that characterize past-to-present time.

3. (You ever taste) _____ such good apple pie?

4. He (still not realize)[15] _____ what a bad mistake he (make)

_____.

5. He is the worst student she (ever have) _____.

6. The baby (sleep) _____ for three hours.

7. He (have) _____ many difficulties since he came to this country.

8. Some students (study) _____ all week for the examination,

while others (not begin) _____ yet.

9. I (knock) _____ on the door for fifteen minutes, but so far no

one (answer) _____.

10. The news about the war (not be) _____ good lately.

11. His admirers (wait) _____ in the rain for two hours just to
see him get off the plane.

12. I (not see) _____ him since last winter.

13. He (recently arrive) _____ in this country.

14. I (never see) _____ such beautiful mountains.

15. He (already finish) _____ his first book, and he (begin)

_____ to work on the second one.

3-15
PRESENT PERFECT PROGRESSIVE TENSE

The present perfect progressive tense is generally used for an action that is viewed as continuous from past to present, with or without repetition.

Wherever possible, change the present perfect verbs to progressive form.

EXAMPLE: a. She has gone to school off and on all her life.
She has been going to school off and on all her life.

b. He has seen a great deal of her lately.
He has been seeing a great deal of her lately.

c. I have seen that movie many times.
(No change possible)

[15]In the present perfect, **still** is used only with the negative. **Still** usually *precedes* the auxiliary.

1. She has said the same thing for an hour.

   _____

2. They have worked on that bridge all year long, but it is still not completed.

   _____

3. The sick boy has not stayed in bed as the doctor ordered.

   _____

4. All day long I have waited for the telegram to arrive.

   _____

5. They have played tennis since early this morning.

   _____

6. He has lived at that hotel a week now.

   _____

7. The tenants have finally paid the rent they owed.

   _____

8. The landlord has promised to fix the leak in the ceiling for a long time.

   _____

9. The same mailman has delivered the mail for ten years.

   _____

10. He has not felt well recently.

   _____

11. The cost of living has risen steadily.

   _____

12. Has he ever written to you since he left town?

   _____

3-16
PRESENT PERFECT TENSE
vs. PAST TENSE

Use the present perfect tense for indefinite time (with **since, for, often, so far, recently,** etc.), or the past tense for definite time (with **yesterday, a few days ago, last week,** etc.). Note where the progressive forms of the verb are possible or preferable. Also note where the past tense may be an informal alternative for the present perfect.

EXAMPLE: a. He (live) <u>has lived</u>, <u>has been living</u> in the same house since he was born.

   b. A plane headed for the West Coast (crash) <u>crashed</u> in the mountains last night.

   c. Her husband (inherit) <u>inherited</u> a lot of money a few years ago.

1. He (not smoke) _____ for several weeks.

2. The girl (fall) _____ off her bicycle many times.

3. He (work) _____ in a factory last summer to earn his tuition for the university.

4. She (be) _____ movie star since she was a child.

5. She (do) _____ her exercises faithfully every day.

6. We (sell) _____ our house several weeks ago.

7. Da Vinci, Michelangelo, Raphael (create) _____ great works of art during the Italian Renaissance.

8. There (be) _____ many accidents on that road recently.

9. Many prominent people (be) _____ in the audience last night.

10. I (have) _____ this toothache since yesterday.

11. He (attend) _____ the university until he ran out of money last year.

12. His business (prosper) _____ so far.

13. Emerson and Thoreau (write) _____ in the 19th century.

14. She (have) _____ the flu last month. She (not feel)

_____ well since.

15. Up to now we (never have) _____ any trouble with our refrigerator.

16. I (not yet see) _____ that play.

17. In the past, more people (live) _____ on farms.

18. He (be) _____ seriously ill for the past few days.

3-17
PAST PERFECT TENSE (1)

The past perfect tense expresses past time that precedes another past time.

> The burglar alarm went off and a crowd began to gather. Soon the police arrived at the scene of the robbery. But they were too late. The thieves **had** already **gone.**

The past perfect tense often occurs in sentences containing dependent clauses.

1. *Adverbial clauses*

> After I had spoken, I realized my mistake.
> Although she had reported the theft immediately, the police were unable to help her.

2. *Adjective clauses*

The man who had stolen the money two weeks ago confessed last night.
The house where he had lived as a child was right on the lake.

3. *Noun clauses*

He said that he had left his wallet at home.
He was worried about what he had just heard.

In each of the following sentences, use a past perfect verb in one of the clauses, and a past verb in the other.

EXAMPLE: a. Before his mother (say) <u>had said</u> one word of reprimand, the child (begin) <u>began</u> to cry.

b. They never (receive) <u>received</u> the books which they (order) <u>had ordered</u>.

c. The police (ask) <u>asked</u> the boy why he (steal) <u>had stolen</u> the money.

1. Almost all the guests (leave) _____ by the time we (arrive)

   _____ .

2. He (never be) _____ ill in his life until he (go)

   _____ into the jungle.

3. He (wonder) _____ whether he (leave)

   _____ his key in the car.

4. The company (not hire) _____ her because she (lie)

   _____ about her past experience.

5. After a while he (realize) _____ that he (take)

   _____ the wrong road.

6. The secretary (not leave) _____ until she (finish)

   _____ her work.

7. They (be married) _____ for five years before any friction

   (arise) _____ between them.

8. When she (finish) _____ her work, she (go)

   _____ to the movies.

9. She (want) _____ to know what (happen)

   _____ at the meeting.

10. The weather (be) _____ far worse than we (expect)

    _____ .

11. By the time we (get) _____ to the airport, our plane (already leave) _____.

12. The girl who (promise) _____ to baby-sit for them (be) _____ too ill to do so.

13. I (not know) _____ that they (move) _____ back to their old home.

14. I (hear) _____ many things about this country before I (come) _____ here.

3-18
PAST PERFECT TENSE (2) WITH *JUST, ALREADY*

In informal speech, the past tense is often used rather than the past perfect tense (**After I spoke, I realized my mistake; The man who stole the money two weeks ago confessed last night; He said he left his wallet at home**). However, in a sentence that contains a past time clause, a main verb accompanied by **just, already, scarcely, barely, no sooner** is usually in the past perfect tense—**She had just washed the windows when it began to rain.**

A. Combine each group of sentences so that the second sentence becomes a **when** clause in the past. Do not use a comma before this time clause at the end of the sentence.

EXAMPLE: a. We (just sit) down to dinner.
A fire (break out) in the kitchen.
We had just sat down to dinner when a fire broke out in the kitchen.

b. He (scarcely begin) to work on his new job.
He (become) seriously ill with pneumonia.
He had scarcely begun to work on his new job when he became seriously ill with pneumonia.

1. He (just buy) a new home.
His company (transfer) him to another city.

_____

_____

2. The examination (already begin).
They (discover) that one page of the examination paper was missing.

_____

_____

3. The student (barely skim) through his new art book.
He (lose) it on the subway.

_____

_____

4. She (already put away) her winter clothes.
   An unseasonable cold spell (force) her to take them out again.

   _____

   _____

5. The company (already ship) the merchandise.
   They (realize) they had sent it to the wrong address.

   _____

   _____

6. He (barely overcome) one financial difficulty.
   Another, more serious one (face) him.

   _____

   _____

7. The couple (scarcely enter) the house.
   They (begin) to argue.

   _____

   _____

8. They (no sooner sell) their car.
   They (regret) having done so.[16]

   _____

   _____

9. They (just hire) a new cook.
   The old one (ask) for her job back.

   _____

   _____

10. The car (hardly go) a mile.
    It (have) a flat tire.

    _____

    _____

11. The guest speaker (no sooner enter) the hall.
    A cheer (arise) from the audience.[16]

    _____

    _____

[16]In formal usage, **no sooner** requires a **than** clause rather than a **when** clause.

B. With **just** and **already,** the past progressive may indicate unfinished past time—**She was just washing the windows when it began to rain.**

Go over the sentences in A to see where the past progressive tense may be used with **just** and **already.**

EXAMPLE: We were just sitting down to dinner when a fire broke out in the kitchen.

3-19
PAST PERFECT PROGRESSIVE TENSE

Whenever possible, change the verbs to progressive form. Keep in mind that the progressive usually emphasizes *duration of a single event.*

EXAMPLE: a. The actor who had played the part of Hamlet became too ill to go on stage.
The actor who had been playing the part of Hamlet became too ill to go on stage.

b. He had never missed a day's performance until he became ill.
(*no change*)

c. He said that he had studied for several hours.
He said that he had been studying for several hours.

1. He had worked for several hours when the mailman came with a special delivery letter.

_____

_____

2. They had discussed several important matters before I got there.

_____

_____

3. We had just sat down to dinner when the doorbell rang.

_____

_____

4. They had planned for a long time to move to the suburbs.

_____

_____

5. He had taken the X-ray treatments up to the time he left.

_____

_____

6. The people who had bought the house next to ours painted it a bright red.

_____

_____

7. They had lived in the slums for several years when I first met them.

_____

_____

8. He said that he had tried to reach us by phone all day long.

_____

_____

9. The store would not refund her money because she had removed the price tag.

_____

_____

10. The children fought for some time before their mother separated them.

_____

_____

3-20
FUTURE PERFECT TENSE

The future perfect tense expresses a future time that precedes another future time. The time indicated by this tense may often begin in the past and have an end point in the future.

The future perfect tense is usually accompanied by a time expression which signals *at, by,* or *before* which time a future event will be completed.

> On the 10th of next month, she will have been a widow for two years.
>
> At the end of this summer, I will (*or* shall) have been away from home for ten years.
>
> When he retires from his work, he will have made more than a million dollars.
>
> By the end of the school year, we will (*or* shall) have covered the entire grammar book.
>
> Before his vacation is over, he will have made many new friends.

Fill in the blanks with the future perfect tense. (Note that many of the time expressions begin with **by**.)

EXAMPLE: a. By the year 2000, this earth (see) <u>will have seen</u> many changes.

b. The taxi (arrive) <u>will have arrived</u> by the time we get downstairs.

1. By the time the rehearsal is over, the audience (begin)

_____ to enter the theater.

2. By next year, he (forget) _____ everything he learned in this class.

3. By the time he is an old man, he (lose) _____ many of his youthful ideals.

4. Next month they (be) _____ in the United States for thirty years.

5. Before he leaves New York, he (go) _____ to every museum in town.

6. By the end of the semester, your English (improve) _____ tremendously.

7. By December, all the leaves (fall) _____ from the trees.

8. On the 26th of next month he (complete) _____ his tour of Europe.

9. By the time you get there, they (rehearse) _____ for ten hours.

10. The political prisoners (escape) _____ from the country by the time their absence is noticed.

11. The leaders of the present regime (help) _____ themselves to a great part of the treasury before they are forced out of power.

12. In ten years time we (pay) _____ off the mortgage on our house.

13. By the time he leaves Las Vegas, he (lose) _____ a great deal of money at the gambling tables.

3-21
PASSIVE FORM OF VERBS (1)

Many verbs may be used to make statements about the same event in two different ways.

Active voice The boy (*subject*) opened the door (*object*).

Passive voice The door (*original object*) was opened by the boy (*original subject*).

Because an original object becomes the grammatical subject in a passive statement, *only transitive verbs*[17] *may be used in the passive voice*. The passive voice requires forms of the verb **be** as tense auxiliaries.

[17]A **transitive** verb is a verb that *takes an object*.

FORMS OF THE
PASSIVE VOICE

Tense	Active Voice		Passive Voice	
Simple present	offer,	offers	am is are }	offered
Present progressive	am is are }	offering	am is are }	being offered
Simple past	offered		was were }	offered
Past progressive	was were }	offering	was were }	being offered
Future	shall will }	offer	shall will }	be offered
Present perfect	have has }	offered	have has }	been offered
Past perfect	had	offered	had	been offered
Future perfect	shall will }	have offered	shall will }	have been offered

The passive voice is preferred when the "doer" of an action (or, the agent) is unimportant or unknown. Because of its impersonal tone, the passive voice is commonly found in textbooks, in scientific, technical or business reports, and in newspaper stories.

Change the following sentences to passive form. Be sure to use the same tense as in the original sentence.

EXAMPLE: a. Their teacher opens the door every morning.

  The door is opened by their teacher every morning.

  (Usually the **by**-phrase agent comes directly after the verb, but there is some flexibility in the word order after the verb.)

  b. Mr. Roberts will paint the murals in the new lecture hall.

  The murals in the new lecture hall will be painted by Mr. Roberts.

  c. His parents punished John for not going to school.

  John was punished by his parents for not going to school.

  d. The board has already discussed the matter.

  The matter has already been discussed by the board.[18]

[18]Adverbs are usually placed after the first auxiliary. In a verb with two auxiliaries, an *-ly* adverb of manner comes after the second auxiliary.

1. The court will try the case next week.
   The case will be tryed by the court next week.

2. His landlord asked him to move.
   He was asked to move by his landlord.

3. The heavy rains are ruining the crops.
   The crops are being ruined by the heavy rains.

4. A garage mechanic recognized the suspected killer.
   The suspected killer was recognized by a garage mechanic.

5. Both houses of Congress have already passed the bill.
   The bill has been passed already by both house of Congress.

6. The fire has entirely destroyed the house.
   The house has been entirely destroyed by fire.

7. The store will deliver the furniture we ordered next week.
   The furniture will be delivered by store next week we ordered next week.

8. All the students respect the new English teacher.

9. His friends have recently given a party in his honor.

10. The repairman is repairing the refrigerator now.

11. A well-known art collector is donating several paintings.

12. The contractors were still building the stadium when a strike halted all construction. (*change both verbs*)

13. Their travel agent will have carefully planned their itinerary long before they start on their trip.

14. A beautiful girl wearing a little white apron was serving the beverages.

_____

_____

3-22
PASSIVE FORM OF VERBS (2)
AGENT OMITTED

The agent is often omitted in passive sentences. In the following sentences containing passive verbs without agents, use the verb form required by the time expression. In some sentences more than one answer is possible.

EXAMPLE: a. The house (paint) every year.

The house is painted every year.

b. The proposal (consider) right now.

The proposal is being considered right now.

c. All the students' grades (distribute) next week.

All the students' grades will be distributed (or are being distributed, are going to be distributed) next week.

d. The matter (already, investigate).

The matter has already been investigated.

1. Much attention (devote) to this question at this time.

_____

2. The furniture (move) tomorrow.

_____

3. A new air conditioner (install) at this very moment.

_____

4. The merchandise (just, ship) when the order was canceled.

_____

5. Their house (paint) when a fire broke out.

_____

6. America (discover) in 1492.

_____

7. Several of the culprits (already, punish).

_____

8.   Today he (know) throughout the world as a great scientist.

_____

9.   Most of the work (complete) before the strike began.

_____

10.   Everything (already, do) to make the patient more comfortable.

_____

11.   All the food (eat) long before we get to the picnic.

_____

12.   Yesterday's parade (lead) by our high school band.

_____

13.   The money which (donate) last week (soon, use) to buy food for the poor.

_____

14.   Her fur coat (just, take) out of storage when it was stolen.

_____

15.   His political activities (investigate) by the government when he vanished from sight.

_____

_____

16.   All the patients (evacuate) from the hospital by the time the enemy forces reach the area.

_____

_____

3-23
PASSIVE OF VERBS
THAT TAKE TWO OBJECTS

With verbs that take indirect objects, either the direct or the indirect object may be the grammatical subject of the passive verb.

Active	The company will give us the guarantee in writing.
Passive	We will be given the guarantee in writing.
	_or_
	The guarantee will be given (to) us in writing.
	(In the passive, **to** is optional with the indirect object after the verb.)

Give the two possible ways of restating the following sentences in the passive. Do not change the tense, and do not include the agent unless it is necessary for the meaning.

EXAMPLE: She sent her husband a telegram.
  <u>Her husband was sent a telegram.</u>
  <u>A telegram was sent (to) her husband.</u>

1. The company gave Mr. Jackson a notice of dismissal.

_____

_____

2. We have mailed them the sample today.

_____

_____

3. The waiter handed him the bill.

_____

_____

4. The hotel is furnishing him everything he needs.

_____

_____

5. The child's aunt had brought him some warm clothes.

_____

_____

6. The teacher will teach the class the next lesson tomorrow.

_____

_____

7. An old resident had told us the whole story.

_____

_____

8. His employer had assigned him too many duties.

_____

_____

9. The bank is lending her the money.

_____

_____

3-24
VERB FORMS IN UNREAL CONDITIONS

Special verb forms are used in sentences that express unreal (contrary-to-fact) conditions. These forms can indicate *present* unreal time or *past* unreal time.

Real condition (future time)	If I **feel** better (a possibility), **I will go** to the movies tonight. (*present* tense with the condition, *future* tense with the *result*)
Unreal condition present time	If I **felt** better (I don't now), **I would go** to the movies. (*past* tense with the condition, the auxiliary *would* with the result)
past time	If I **had felt** better (I didn't yesterday), I **would have gone** to the movies. (*past perfect* tense with the condition, the auxiliaries *would have* with the result)

Use the following real situations to make sentences with *present* or *past* unreal conditions. Watch for negative-positive changes.

	Real situation	*Result*
EXAMPLE: a.	I don't have a car now.	I won't take a drive in the country.
	If I had a car now, I would take a drive in the country.	
b.	I didn't have a car last week.	I didn't take a drive in the country.
	If I had had a car last week, I would have taken a drive in the country.	

	Real situation	*Result*
1.	I don't earn enough money now.	I won't buy a large house.
2.	I didn't earn enough money last year.	I didn't buy a house.
3.	He doesn't try hard.	He won't succeed.
4.	He didn't try hard when he was in school.	He didn't succeed.
5.	I can't swim.	I won't go swimming with you.

6.	I didn't know you were in town yesterday.	I didn't invite you to dinner.
7.	I'm not at home now.[19]	I'm not watching television.
8.	I didn't have time last night.	I didn't go to the discothèque.
9.	She doesn't know how to use the computer.	She doesn't use it in her work.
10.	I didn't read the textbook carefully.	I failed my course in psychology.
11.	There isn't enough paper.	I can't finish this report.[20]
12.	You didn't give the plants enough water.	They died.

3-25
NEGATIVES OF VERBS

Verbs are made negative by adding **not** to them. The position of **not** depends on the number of auxiliaries with the verb.

Verbs with no auxiliaries (simple present and simple, past tense only)					
be	*Mary* **is** *late*.	*Mary*	*is*	*not*		*late*.
all other verbs	*Mary* **arrived** *late*.	*Mary*	*did* (aux. added)	*not*	*arrive*	*late*.
Verbs with 1–3 auxiliaries					
1 aux.	*Mary* **has arrived** *late*.	*Mary*	*has*	*not*	*arrived*	*late*.
2–3 aux.	*Mary* **has been arriving** *late*.	*Mary*	*has*	*not*	*been arriving*	*late*.

Negative contractions are made by combining an auxiliary (or a single form of **be, have**) with **not** and by using an apostrophe for the **o** that is omitted from **not.**

Examples: have + nøt = haven't
was + nøt = wasn't
do + nøt = don't
should + nøt = shouldn't

[19]Formally, **were** is the past form used in unreal conditions. Informally, **was** is frequently heard.
[20]**Could** may be used as well as **would** in a result clause.

Some contractions are irregular:

$$can + n\emptyset t = can't$$
$$will + n\emptyset t = won't$$

There is a tendency to avoid the contractions **mayn't** and **mightn't.** Shan't a contraction of **shall** and **not,** is not common in American usage.

The use of a double negative, once with the verb and once elsewhere in the sentence, is considered unacceptable.

unacceptable   **I don't have no more money.**
corrected to   **I don't have any more money.**
                or **I have no more money.**

Contractions are common in conversational English but are generally avoided in formal English.

Make the following sentences negative. Use contractions with **not.**

Verbs with No Auxiliaries

1. John is handsome.

   _____

2. The children are eager to go camping.

   _____

3. It is very cold today.

   _____

4. There is enough food for everyone.

   _____

5. They were at home yesterday.

   _____

6. She was curious about his being there.

   _____

7. He drove to work today.

   _____

8. She tells many lies.

   _____

9. Some people like a warm climate.

   _____

10. They have a lot of money today.[21]

_____

11. They had a lot of money last week.

_____

12. We have to make an immediate decision.

_____

Verbs with One Auxiliary

1. They are arriving next week.

_____

2. The students were behaving very well.

_____

3. His money will last forever.

_____

4. He has found a suitable place to live.

_____

5. They have invited us to lunch.

_____

6. He can play tennis very well.

_____

7. We must close all the windows.

_____

8. The instruments have already arrived.[22]

_____

Verbs with Two to Three Auxiliaries

1. His political campaign is being financed by his friends.

_____

2. The doors will be opened before noon.

_____

[21]In negatives and questions, the simple present tense of **have** meaning *possess* may occur with or without the auxiliary **do.**
[22]**Already** becomes **yet** in a negative; in a question **yet** is more common but **already** is sometimes possible.

3. The money should be left in the cash register at night.

_____

4. The concert will have begun by 8 P.M.

_____

5. They might have moved from their old house.

_____

6. Car owners have been warned to lock their cars.

_____

3-26
YES-NO QUESTIONS

		Subject	Balance of predicate	
Verbs with no auxiliaries (simple present and simple past only)				
be	Mary **is** late.	*Is*	*Mary*		*late?*
all other verbs	Mary **arrived** late.	*Did* (aux. added.)	*Mary*	*arrive*	*late?*
Verbs with 1–3 auxiliaries				
1 aux.	Mary **has arrived** late.	*Has*	*Mary*	*arrived*	*late?*
2-3 aux.	Mary **has been arriving** late.	*Has*	*Mary*	*been arriving*	*late?*

Short answers to yes-no questions consist of: (1) a personal pronoun referring to the subject of the sentence, and (2) the verb form that starts the question.

Is Mary late?	Yes, she **is.**	*or*	No, she **isn't.**
Did Mary arrive late?	Yes, she **did.**	*or*	No, she **didn't.**
Has Mary arrived late?	Yes, she **has.**	*or*	No, she **hasn't.**
Has Mary been arriving late?	Yes, she **has.**	*or*	No, she **hasn't.**

Only **there** and impersonal **it** may also be used in a short answer to a **yes-no** question.

Are **there** enough chairs?	Yes, **there** are.	*or*	No, **there** aren't.
Is **it** raining?	Yes, **it** is.	*or*	No, **it** isn't.

In short answers, contractions are not made between the subject and the verb.

Change the sentences in Exercise 3-25 (pp. 79–81) to yes-no questions and give the short answers.

EXAMPLE: a. Is John handsome? Yes, he is. or No, he isn't.

b. Are they arriving next week? Yes, they are. or No, they aren't.

Negative Yes-No Questions

In negative questions, contractions with **not** are generally used.

Isn't Mary late?

Didn't Mary **arrive** late?

Hasn't Mary **arrived** late?

Hasn't Mary **been arriving** late?

In more formal style without the contraction, **not** appears after the reversed verb-subject—
Is Mary **not** late?

Change the sentences in Exercise 3-25 (pp. 79–81) to negative questions.

EXAMPLE: a. Isn't John handsome?

b. Aren't they arriving next week?

Informal Omission of Auxiliaries of Yes-No Questions

In highly informal conversation, the initial auxiliary (or the independent verb **be**) and the subject **you** are sometimes omitted from a yes-no question.

Need any money?	*for* Do you need any money?
Found an apartment yet?	*for* Have you found an apartment yet?
Going with us tonight?	*for* Are you going with us tonight?

Supply the words that are "understood" in the following informal yes-no questions. Give short answers to these questions.

EXAMPLE: a. Do you want to go to the movies?
Yes, I do, or No, I don't.

b. Have you received the money yet?
Yes, I have, or No, I haven't.

c. Are you excited about your trip?
Yes, I am, or No, I'm not.

1. _____ get the tickets?

_____

2. _____ ready to go soon?

_____

3. _____ drive to work today?

_____

4. _____ anything wrong with this typewriter?[23]

_____

5. _____ told her the good news yet?

_____

6. _____ ever play tennis or badminton?

_____

7. _____ studying hard these days?

_____

8. _____ hear any more news about your scholarship?

_____

9. _____ had any luck lately at the horse races?

_____

10. _____ ever gone to the opera?

_____

11. _____ expecting someone?

_____

12. _____ ever find your wallet?

_____

3-27
QUESTIONS WITH INTERROGATIVE WORDS

Questions Beginning with
Interrogative Adverbs—*Why? When?*
Where? How?

Interrogative Adverb	Auxiliary (or **be**)	Subject	Balance of Predicate	
Why	*is*	*Mary*		*late?*
Why	*did* (aux. added)	*Mary*	*arrive*	*late?*
Why	*has*	*Mary*	*arrived*	*late?*
Why	*has*	*Mary*	*been arriving*	*late?*

[23]The expletive **there** may be omitted in this kind of question.

How may combine with an adjective or adverb:

> How tall are you?
> How expensive is that dress?
> How quickly can you get here?
> How badly was he hurt?

There are two informal equivalents of **why**:

what. . .for	What did you do that for?
how come (very informal)	How come you came so late?
	(**How come** may also be interpreted as "how does it happen that."

Informally, some questions with **why** may omit the auxiliary and the subject.

> There is a fine beach nearby. Why go (= should you go) to a beach farther away?
> The plan may work. Why not give (= don't you give) it a chance?

A. Change the following sentences into as many questions as you can that begin with **when, where, why, how,** or **how** + an adjective or adverb. Make sure that these interrogative adverbs are *followed by a verb* (the independent verb **be** or an auxiliary).

EXAMPLE: a. Helen was studying in the main library for three hours.

Where was Helen for three hours?

How long was Helen in the library?

  b. Marie has recently borrowed $1,000 to pay for her tuition.

When has Marie borrowed $1,000 to pay for her tuition?

Why has Marie borrowed $1,000?

What has Marie recently borrowed $1,000 for?

  c. The student from Japan is frequently absent because of illness.

Why is the student from Japan frequently absent?

How often is the student from Japan absent?

1. Luis is from Venezuela.

_____

_____

2. Mary's friend goes to the theater once a week.

_____

_____

3. The Taylors returned the lawn mower to their neighbors right away.

_____

_____

4. Mr. Smith gave his wife a beautiful ring for her birthday.

_____

_____

5. Clara played tennis with Bob yesterday.

_____

_____

6. Everyone at the meeting was asked to contribute money for the poor.

_____

_____

7. Leo's employer is planning a big celebration in an expensive restaurant.

_____

_____

8. The girl is taking her younger brother to the movies.

_____

_____

9. The front door should be carefully locked when you leave the house.

_____

_____

10. She went to the bakery for bread. (*include* **what . . . for**)

_____

_____

11. All the volunteers must report to the personnel office immediately.

_____

_____

12. His wife's new coat cost $150.

_____

_____

13. Mr. Anderson will put half of his salary in the bank today.

_____

_____

14. Mr. Brown's secretary went to the post office to get some stamps. (*include* **what . . . for**)

_____

_____

15. George will travel to the West Coast by bus.

_____

_____

16. She can type fifty words a minute.

_____

_____

17. Their son is five years old.

_____

_____

18. His uncle sends him an expensive gift every year.

_____

_____

Questions Beginning with Interrogative Pronouns

1. **Who** (**whom** for object, **whose** for possessive)—for persons
2. **What**—for things
3. **Which**—for persons or things, when a choice is involved

Interrogative pronoun as:				
object of verb	**Whom**	**do**	**you**	**want?** (*Informal*—Who do you want?)
	What	**can**	**I**	**do for you?**
object of preposition	**To whom**	**is**	**be**	**speaking?** (*informal*—Who(m) is he speaking to?)
	On what	**will**	**he**	**lecture?** (*informal*—What will he lecture on?)
subject of verb			*Who*	**invented the telephone?**
			What	**has caused the accident?**

Note that only questions with interrogative *subjects* do not reverse the subject and the verb.

The preceding informal choices are very common in conversational English.

B. Change the sentences in A on pp. 84–86 into as many questions as you can using the interrogative pronouns **who** (or **whom, whose**), **what, which**. Note the informal as well as the formal choices.

EXAMPLE: a. *Who was studying in the main library for three hours?* ALSO *What was Helen doing in the main library for three hours? Do is a generalized substitute word for an activity, especially when used in a question.*

b. *Who has recently borrowed $1,000 to pay for her tuition? What has Marie recently borrowed to pay for her tuition?*

c. *Who is frequently absent because of illness?*

3-28
QUESTIONS WITH
INTERROGATIVE ADJECTIVES
WHOSE, WHAT, WHICH

Interrogative Adjective With:

subject	**What** guarantee comes with this television set? **Which** bus goes to Main Street?
object	**What** guarantee can you give? **Which** bus shall I take?
object of preposition	From **whose** garden did you get these flowers? To **which** post office should this be taken? On **what** grounds are you suing him?

Based on the italicized phrases, form questions using **whose, what, which** as interrogative adjectives. Keep in mind that **which** implies a choice (of persons or of things), **what** merely asks for information. Note also where **when** or **where** may replace a phrase with a preposition.

EXAMPLE: a. He is taking *the 10:30 bus.*
Which bus is he taking?

b. He is taking a vacation *on his doctor's advice.*
On whose advice is he taking a vacation?

c. He is arriving *at 5 o'clock.*
At what time is he arriving? (At may be omitted.)

or When is he arriving?

1. *Mr. Smith's store* is going to be sold.

---

2. They live *on 72nd Street.*

---

3. They sat *in the last row*.

_____

4. They are going to transplant *the tree on the front lawn*.

_____

5. *His father's friend* scolded him.

_____

6. *All the students* were punished.

_____

7. *Pan-American Airlines* has a flight at that time.

_____

8. She's wearing *her sister's sweater*.

_____

9. They canceled the play *because the star became ill*. (Use **for what reason.**)

_____

10. The parade will begin *at 10:00* A.M.

_____

3-29
ATTACHED QUESTIONS

This kind of yes-no question consists of two parts. The first part makes a *statement;* the second part asks the question that expects agreement with the statement. The second part contains the regular question auxiliary plus the personal pronoun that stands for the subject (or the expletives **it, there**).

Statement	+	Attached Question	Expected Answer
Mary **is** late,		**is'nt** she?	Yes, she is.
Mary **isn't** late,		**is** she?	No, she isn't.
Mary **arrived** late,		**didn't** she?	Yes, she did.
Mary **didn't** arrive late,		**did** she?	No, she didn't.
Mary **has** arrived late,		**hasn't** she?	Yes, she has.
Mary **hasn't** arrived late,		**has** she?	No, she hasn't.
Mary **has** been arriving late,		**hasn't** she?	Yes, she has.
Mary **hasn't** been arriving late,		**has** she?	No, she hasn't.

Note that the attached part of the question begins with the same auxiliary (or the independent verb **be**) as the simple yes-no question. Note also that each question contains a positive-negative or a negative-positive contrast.

Change the following statements into attached questions expecting (1) the answer *yes,* (2) the answer *no.* Give the expected short answers.

EXAMPLE:　a.　The girl remembers you.

　　　　　　The girl remembers you, doesn't she? Yes, she does.

　　　　　　The girl doesn't remember you, does she? No, she doesn't.

　　　　　b.　There is a piano in the room.

　　　　　　There is a piano in the room, isn't there? Yes, there is.

　　　　　　There isn't a piano in the room, is there? No, there isn't.

1. Mr. Brown is rich.

_____

_____

2. Janice broke her arm.

_____

_____

3. The coffee will be ready soon.

_____

_____

4. He has been having financial trouble.

_____

_____

5. The post office is far from here.

_____

_____

6. It is cold outside.

_____

_____

7. You take cream with your coffee.

_____

_____

8. The reservations have already been made.[24]

_____

_____

[24]**Already** becomes **yet** in a negative sentence.

9. There were many people in the room.

_____

_____

10. The calendars have been ordered.

_____

_____

11. He can come with us.

_____

_____

12. They could have left the office early.[25]

_____

_____

13. There is someone at the door.[26]

_____

_____

14. It is beginning to snow.

_____

_____

15. The police caught the thief.

_____

_____

16. We have to fill out these forms.

_____

_____

REVIEW OF VERBS

A. Use the correct form of the verb. Observe formal usage but note informal choices.

1. The milk _____ (taste) sour.

2. She (try) _____ to finish her work early today.

3. It (get) _____ colder and colder these days.

[25]Sometimes **have** as a second auxiliary is included in a short answer—**Yes, they could have.**
[26]**Some** becomes **any** in a negative sentence.

4. I (hear) _____ some loud noises right now.

5. He (listen) _____ to the radio at the moment.

6. I (see) _____ some children outside now.

7. I (watch) _____ the children play outside now.

8. He (admire) _____ his father very much. (general statement)

9. She (spend) _____ too much money on clothes. (general statement)

10. He (work) _____ in a restaurant the last time I saw him.

11. Shakespeare (write) _____ his great plays many years ago.

12. He (call) _____ you tomorrow.

13. I (live) _____ here since 1963.

14. The news about the war (be) _____ good lately.

15. I (visit) _____ that museum three times so far.

16. I (not see) _____ him since last winter.

17. She (have) _____ the flu last month. She (not feel) _____ well since.

18. Up to now we (never have) _____ any trouble with our refrigerator.

19. He (never be) _____ ill in his life until he (go) _____ into the jungle.

20. He wondered whether he (leave) _____ his wallet at home.

21. After a while she realized that she (take) _____ the wrong road.

22. By the time we got to the airport, our plane (already leave) _____.

23. He (just buy) _____ a new home when his company (transfer) _____ him to another city.

24. The student (barely skim) _____ through his new art book when he (lose) _____ it on the subway.

25. The company (already ship) _____ the merchandise when they (realize) _____ they had sent it to the wrong address.

26. By next year, she (forget) _____ everything she learned in this class.

27. Next month she (be) _____ in the United States for thirty years.

28. By December, all the leaves (fall) _____ from the trees.

29. The case (try) _____ by the court next month.

30. The new English teacher (respect) _____ by the students.

31. The car (repair) _____ by the mechanic now.

32. America (discover) _____ in 1492.

33. All the students' grades (distribute) _____ next week.

34. Yesterday's parade (lead) _____ by our high school band.

35. Several of the culprits (already, punish) _____.

36. The furniture (move) _____ tomorrow.

37. Most of the work (complete) _____ before the strike began.

B. Use the *past tense* or the *past participle* of the irregular verbs in parentheses. (*Only one word* is required for each sentence.)

1. The ship (sink) _____ some time ago.

2. They (freeze) _____ the food before they shipped it.

3. The letter was (write) _____ last night.

4. Have you ever (speak) _____ to him about this matter?

5. The girl has just (fall) _____ off her bicycle and (hurt) _____ herself.

6. Many planes (fly) _____ over the city yesterday.

7. He has (swear) _____ to get revenge on the man who attacked him.

8. Her dress was (tear) _____ on a nail.

9. She (bite) _____ her tongue while she was chewing on her steak.

10. These dresses should be (take) _____ to the dry cleaner's.

11. He (hide) _____ the money a few days ago.

12. She has (lie) _____ in bed all day.

13. They (shake) _____ hands warmly as they parted.

14. The notice was (stick) _____ up on the bulletin board.

15. A bee (sting) _____ him in the arm while he was in the garden.

16. The soldiers were (lead) _____ by their captain.

17. Many women have (weep) _____ for their husbands who were killed in battle.

18. The children have already been (feed) _____ .

19. It was (think) _____ that the thief had not gone far.

20. The news has already been (spread) _____ all over town.

C. Change the following sentences to the *passive* voice. Do not omit the agent. In some cases *two* passive sentences should be given.

1. A garage mechanic recognized the suspected killer.

_____

2. The repairman is repairing the refrigerator now.

_____

3. The court will try the case next month.

_____

4. The bank is lending her the money.

_____

5. The government was investigating his political activities.

_____

6. The new clerk might have stolen her umbrella.

_____

7. The waiter handed him the bill.

_____

D. Make questions for which the italicized words are the answers.

1. Mr. Smith gave his wife a beautiful ring *for her birthday*.

_____

2. Clara played tennis with *Bob* yesterday.

_____

3. Leo's employer is planning a big celebration *in an expensive restaurant*.

_____

4. His wife's new coat cost *$150*.

_____

5. George will travel to the West Coast *by bus*.

_____

6. They are going to transplant *the tree on the front lawn*.

_____

7. *His father's friend* scolded him.

_____

E. Change the sentences to *attached questions* (with two parts) expecting (a) the answer *yes*, and (b) the answer *no*. Give the expected answers.

EXAMPLE: a. You can come, can't you? Yes, I can. (Attached question expecting *yes*.)

b. She doesn't know any English, does she? No, she doesn't. (Attached question expecting *no*)

1. Janice broke her arm.

_____

_____

2. The plane will arrive soon.

_____

_____

3. The calendars have been ordered.

_____

_____

4. There were many people in the room.

_____

_____

5. We have to fill out these forms.

_____

_____

6. The reservations have already been made.

_____

_____

7. There is someone at the door.

_____

_____

4

Auxiliaries

Types of Auxiliaries

Tense				
Tense	**be**	+	**-ing** present participle for *progressive* forms	He *is opening* the door now.
	be	+	**-ed** past participle[1] for *passive* forms	Many soldiers *were wounded* in the battle.
	have	+	**-ed** past participle for the *perfect* tenses[1]	They *have* just *arrived.*
	shall–will	+	simple form of the verb for the *future* tense	They *will arrive* soon.
Questions, negatives of auxiliary-less verbs	**do**	+	simple form of verb	*Did* he *arrive* on time? He *didn't arrive* on time.
Modal	can–could may–might should would must be able to[2] ought to[2] have to[2] }	+	simple form of verb	He *can* *should* } speak English. *must*
	These modal auxiliaries add a special meaning such as *ability, permission, possibility,* etc., to the meaning of the main part of the verb.			

[1]The regular ending for the past participle is **-ed.** See Chapter 3 for the irregular forms of past participles (third principal part).

[2]It is customary to include these verbs followed by **to** among the modals not only because they have the same meanings as the modals listed here but also because they form negatives and questions in the same way as modal auxiliaries do.

A verb with an auxiliary is usually made negative by placing **not** after the auxiliary.

The first exercises in this chapter will be concerned with the forms of verb phrases containing auxiliaries; the next exercises will concentrate mainly on the special meanings of the modal auxiliaries.

4-1
VERB FORMS WITH ONE AUXILIARY

| am
is
are
was
were } | **offering** (progressive)
or
offered (passive) | have
has
had } | **offered** (perfect) | do–does–did
shall–should
will–would
can–could
may–might
must } | **offer** |

Use the correct form of the verb.

EXAMPLE: a. They are (open) <u>opening</u> the store right now.

b. All these houses were (sell) <u>sold</u> last year.

c. We have finally (finish) <u>finished</u> the work.

d. We can (be) <u>be</u> there at five o'clock.

1. The windows were (clean) _____ yesterday.

2. She is (study) _____ very hard this year.

3. She has (choose) _____ a fine profession.

4. He should (arrive) _____ in a few hours.

5. They were (argue) _____ bitterly when I met them.

6. He has (mislay) _____ the money somewhere.

7. They might (visit) _____ us tomorrow.

8. The hunter was (attack) _____ by a bear.

9. I would (appreciate) _____ it if you would keep quiet.

10. The bills were (pay) _____ last week.

11. She has (bring) _____ her children with her.

12. The two men were already (fight) _____ when the police came.

13. The thief was (catch) _____ a few hours ago.

14. Her jewelry is (keep) _____ in a locked drawer.

15. Are the books still (lie) _____ on the table?

16. Have they (dig) _____ the foundation yet?

17. Were they (permit) _____ to leave the country?

18. Shall I (serve) _____ the dinner now?[3]

4-2

VERB FORMS WITH TWO AUXILIARIES (1)
BE, BEEN, BEING AS THE SECOND AUXILIARY

A. Active Progressive (with -ING Participle)

Present Form of First Auxiliary		Past Form of First Auxiliary	
have has	**been offering**	had	**been offering**
will shall can may must	**be offering**	would should could might	**be offering**

Use the correct form of the **progressive.** (The first auxiliary is already given with each verb.)

EXAMPLE: a.   They (will leave will be leaving for London tomorrow.

b.   Guests (have come) have been coming in and out all day today.

c.   (He, has lived) Has he been living in the same house all of his life?

1. I (shall stay) _____ at my friends' house next week.

2. You (can do) _____ your homework while I get dinner ready.

3. I don't know where my husband is; he (may visit) _____ one of our neighbors.

4. My secretary isn't at her desk; she (must take) _____ her afternoon break.

5. They told us that they (had waited) _____ for more than two hours.

6. He (would go) _____ to the university now if his father hadn't lost his money in the stock market.

[3]**Shall** used in this kind of question is the equivalent of **Do you want me to, Would you like me to?**

7. The play (should end) _____ soon; it's almost 11:00 P.M.

8. The enemy (could prepare) _____ for a new attack; intelligence sources report that increased supplies are being brought in.

9. Let's take an umbrella; it (might rain) _____ when we get out of the theater.

10. He (will come) _____ in on the six o'clock train.

11. (He, has caused) _____ any more disturbances in school?

12. (The plants, should get) _____ more water?

B. Passive (with -ED Participle)[4]

Present Form of the First Auxiliary	Past Form of First Auxiliary
have has } **been offered**	had **been offered**
am is are } **being offered**	was were } **being offered**
will shall can may must } **be offered**	would should could might } **be offered**

Use the correct form of the **passive voice.** (The first auxiliary is already given with each verb.)

EXAMPLE: a. The troops (have instructed) <u>have been instructed</u> to get ready to leave at once.

b. The doors (will open) <u>will be opened</u> at 10:00 A.M.

c. (He might stop) <u>Might, he be stopped</u> if he tries to cross the border?

1. We (shall sue) _____ by the landlord if we don't pay the back rent at once.

2. The job (can finish) _____ on time if all the employees work overtime for a few days.

3. All traffic violators (shall fine)[5] _____ heavily.

4. All parcels (must wrap) _____ so that they (may open) _____ for postal inspection.

5. The children (be served) _____ dinner when some of their friends came to see them.

[4]The expression *-ed participle* is used in this book to refer to all past participles, whether they are regular or not.
[5]**Shall** used with the third person often represents legal or commercial usage.

6. He (had just made) _____ a partner in his law firm when he suffered a severe heart attack.

7. If the boy returned to his family, he (would forgive) _____ for running away.

8. The superintendent of the building (should notify) _____ in case of any emergency.

9. If he were here now, that problem (could solve) _____ easily.

10. If he (had offered) _____ a gift, he would have refused it.

11. The books which (must read) _____ by the students in the

    class (have listed) _____ on the sheet which (be handed out)

    _____ now.

12. (He, should allow) _____ to do whatever he pleases?

13. (These items, are put) _____ on sale tomorrow?

14. This letter (must retype) _____; there are too many errors in it.

15. (They, will offend) _____ if we don't come to their party?

16. (The office, has notified) _____ of his illness?

4-3
VERB FORMS WITH TWO AUXILIARIES (2)
HAVE AS THE SECOND AUXILIARY

Active Voice (with -ED Participle)

Present Form of First Auxiliary	Past Form of First Auxiliary
will shall can[6] may must ⎬ **have offered**	would should could might ⎬ **have offered**

Note that **have** as the second auxiliary never changes its form.

Use the correct form of the verb with *have* **as the second auxiliary.**

EXAMPLE: a. They (will leave) <u>will have left</u> the city long before we get there.

            b. She (must be) <u>must have been</u> in a great hurry to leave for the theater because she left all the dinner dishes on the table.

            c. (The accident, might occur) <u>Might the accident have occurred</u> as he described it?

[6]**Can have offered** is not commonly used.

1. That store has just gone bankrupt. I believe they (should have)

   _____ a stricter policy about giving people credit.

2. That store (might not go) _____ bankrupt if they had had a stricter policy about giving people credit.

3. I can't find my keys; I (may leave) _____ them at home.

4. We (would meet) _____ you at the station if we had known you were coming.

5. The plants (must die) _____ because no one watered them.

6. Next week, the painters (will be) _____ on strike for half a year.

7. They (must lose) _____ a great deal of money in the stock market.

8. He (would win) _____ the tennis match if he had not sprained his ankle.

9. If you had done those exercises, you (might benefit) _____ from them.

10. (He, might plan) _____ the whole thing himself?

11. We (shall travel) _____ a thousand miles by the end of the month.

12. The children in this school (will learn) _____ to read well by the time they are seven years old.

13. If he had wanted to, (he, could send) _____ the money?

4-4
VERB FORMS WITH THREE AUXILIARIES
HAVE AS THE SECOND AUXILIARY

A. Active Progressive (with -ING Participle)

Present Form of First Auxiliary	Past Form of First Auxiliary
will shall can[7] may must } **have been offering**	would should could might } **have been offering**

[7]**Can have been offering** is not commonly used.

Use the correct form of the **progressive** with *have* **as the second auxiliary.** Remember that **have** as the second auxiliary never changes.

EXAMPLE: He (may steal) <u>may have been stealing</u> for a long time without his parents knowing about it.

1. He (must sleep) _____ so soundly that he didn't hear the alarm go off.

2. They (will rehearse) _____ for an hour by the time we get there.

3. On November 20, I (shall do) _____ the same work for thirty years.

4. The girl (may smoke) _____ for some time before her mother caught her doing it.

5. We're sorry our plane is so late in arriving. You (must wait) _____ a long time.

6. You (should not watch) _____ television last night if you had so much homework.

7. You (would live) _____ in luxury for some time if you had taken your stockbroker's advice.

8. Those men (must smuggle) _____ in the jewelry for several years before they were caught.

9. He (should save) _____ for the future instead of spending all his money on luxuries.

10. He (could not work) _____ at that time, because he was just recovering from a serious operation.

11. Only those personnel that had access to the telegraph (could send) _____ the messages to the enemy.

12. He (must do) _____ extremely well in his schoolwork, because he was offered scholarships from several fine universities.

13. The thieves (must watch) _____ the house for some time before they broke into it.

B. Passive Voice (with -ED Participle)

Present Form of First Auxiliary		Past Form of First Auxiliary	
will shall can[8] may must }	**have been offered**	would should could might }	**have been offered**

[8]**Can have been offered** is not commonly used.

Use the correct form of the **passive** with *have* **as the second auxiliary.** Remember that **have** as the second auxiliary never changes.

EXAMPLE: a. For all we know, the child (may abandon) <u>may have been abandoned</u> by his mother some time ago.

b. The money (would send) <u>would have been sent</u> to you at once if we had known your address.

c. (The fire, might start) <u>Might the fire have been started</u> by an arsonist?

1. Surely the package (will receive) _____ by now.

2. The door (must leave) _____ open, because the thief seems to have entered the house without any difficulty.

3. They (should inform) _____ by the company that their insurance was about to expire.

4. The automobile accident (could prevent) _____ if he had been more alert.

5. The gangster (might shoot) _____ by a rival gangster.

6. Thousands of people (must kill) _____ by the eruptions of Mt. Vesuvius.

7. The bill (would veto) _____ by the President if certain changes had not been made in it.

8. The rehearsal (must cancel) _____ because the theater is dark.

9. He (should allow) _____ to say a few words in his defense.

10. The car (should not drive) _____ so fast in that heavy traffic.

11. The burning building (may strike) _____ by lightning.

12. (The letter, might write) _____ by the mayor himself?

13. (The injured man could strike) _____ by a heavy object?

4-5
REVIEW OF AUXILIARY FORMS

A. Use the Correct Form of the *Progressive.*

1. You (can do) _____ your homework while I get dinner ready.

2. They (will rehearse) _____ for an hour by the time we get there.

3. My secretary isn't at her desk; she (must take) _____ her afternoon break.

4. They told me that they (have waited) _____ for more than two hours.

5. The girl (may smoke) _____ for some time before her mother caught her doing it.

6. You (should do) _____ your homework last night instead of watching television.

7. The play (should end) _____ soon; it's almost 11:00 P.M.

8. He (will come) _____ in on the six o'clock train.

9. She (study) _____ very hard this year.

10. He (must sleep) _____ so soundly that he didn't hear the alarm go off.

11. He (should save) _____ for the future instead of spending all his money on luxuries.

12. They (argue) _____ when I met them.

B. Use the Correct Form of the *Passive.*

1. The children (be served) _____ dinner when some of their friends came to see them.

2. The superintendent of the building (should notify) _____ in case of any emergency.

3. All parcels (must wrap) _____ so that they (may open) _____ for postal inspection.

4. The money (would send) _____ to you at once if we had known your address.

5. The door (must leave) _____ open, because the thief seems to have entered the house without any difficulty.

6. If he were here now, that problem (could solve) _____ easily.

7. This letter (must retype) _____; there are too many errors in it.

8. What do you think (should do) _____ to settle the newspaper strike?

9. The automobile accident (could prevent) _____ if we had been more alert.

10. Thousands of people (must kill) _____ by the eruptions of Mt. Vesuvius.

11. The gangster (might shoot) _____ by a rival gangster.

12. He (should allow) _____ to say a few words in his defense.

Physical ability	I can (*or* am able to) lift this stone.
Learned ability	She can (*or* is able to) type.
Have the power to	I can see you tonight.
	This factory can produce dozens of machines a day.

It is only in this third sense of ability (which is related to possibility), that **can** and, to a lesser extent **be able to,** may refer to future time. **Be able to** is generally not used with a passive verb.

Use the correct form of can and be able to (where possible).

EXAMPLE: a. When I was a boy, I (speak) <u>could speak</u> *or* <u>was able to speak</u> several foreign languages, but now I (speak) <u>can speak</u> *or* <u>am able to speak</u> only one foreign language.

  b. This error (correct) <u>can be corrected</u> easily.

1. No one (go) _____ without sleep indefinitely.

2. (You, reach) _____ the top shelf of the cabinet?

3. She (swim) _____ several miles without getting tired.

4. He (not paint) _____ the whole house in one day.

5. This kind of dress (make) _____ with very little material.

6. The bank repossessed his car because he (not keep up)[9]

   _____ his payments.

7. (You, have) _____ dinner with me tonight?

8. The car ran out of gas, so they (not go) _____ any farther.

9. Why (you, not lend) _____ him some money last week?

10. John thought he (pass) _____ the examination.

11. That matter (settle) _____ only by heads of state.

12. (The typist, finish) _____ all the letters today?

13. The error (correct) _____ very easily.

14. He said that he (move) _____ the piano without any help.

15. My watch is very old; it (not repair) _____ any more.

[9]If the main verb is past (**repossessed**), the other verbs in the sentence are usually past also (sequence of tenses).

	Question (Requesting Permission)	Permission Being Granted
First person	May (*or* can) I borrow your car?	You may (*or* can) borrow my car if you drive carefully.
Third person	May (*or* can) John come to the movies with us?	Yes, John may go to the movies with you.

Can used for permission is considered informal. The past forms of **may** and **can** are also used in requests—**Might** (or **could**) **I borrow your car.**[10]

May or **can** are also used in the sense of *be permitted*. In this sense, the past forms **might** and **could** express only past time.

Present or "timeless" time	Anyone may (*or* can) enroll in this course.
Past time	In those days, anyone might (*or* could) enroll for the course.

In the sequence of tenses **might** and **could** also indicate only past time.

Present time	John's mother **says** that he **may** (*or* **can**) go with us.
Past time	John's mother **said** that he **might** (*or* **could**) go with us.

Use the correct form of may or can.

EXAMPLE: a. (I, see) <u>May I see</u> *or* Can I see you tonight?

        b. (I, permit) <u>May I be permitted</u> to look for the book myself?

1. (I, come) _____ in?

2. (I, help) _____ you carry those packages?

3. (I, leave) _____ the office a little early today?

4. (The children, come over) _____ to play with my children?

5. Yes, they _____ , if they are back by dinner time.

[10]Where there is a choice between a present or past modal, the past form usually lessens the force of the modal.

6. Anyone (attend) _____ our church services.

7. Our teacher told us we (take) _____ one hour off to do some research in the library.

8. Students (attend) _____ the performance free if they get their tickets in advance.

9. Anyone who has a library card (take out) _____ books from the library.

10. (I, be excused) _____ from class early today?

11. Until recently, anyone (enter) _____ the factory without permission.

4-8
OBLIGATION, ADVISABILITY
SHOULD, OUGHT TO, HAD BETTER

Should, ought to, had better occur in statements about one's duty or advantage, which one is free to accept or reject.

1. *Obligation* (What one is expected to do)—**You should (*or* ought to) do your homework every day.**
2. *Advisability* (What is wise for one to do)—**She should (*or* ought to, *or* had better) eat less if she wants to lose weight.**

The forms used for past time, **should have, ought to have,** imply that the action did not occur. (**Ought to have** is often avoided because of its awkwardness.)

Had better is a past form used for present time. It refers to past time only in sequence of tenses—*He thought he had better attend the meeting.* **Had better** may also express a warning—*You had better stay off my property, or I'll have you arrested.*

A. Use both **should** and **ought to** where possible. Use the correct form of the auxiliary.

EXAMPLE: a. Everyone (go) <u>should go</u> (*or* <u>ought to go</u>) to the dentist once a year.

b. Mr. Johnson (go) <u>should have gone</u> (*or* <u>ought to have gone</u>) to the dentist yesterday, but he was too busy. (Mr. Johnson didn't go to the dentist.)

1. You (help) _____ your mother with the housework.

2. I (write) _____ some letters tonight, but I have a headache.

3. The air conditioner (clean) _____ once a year.

4. The question is whether he (allow) _____ to hold two jobs at once.

5. Everyone (save) _____ for a rainy day.

6. We (not leave) _____ the door unlocked when we left the house.

7. The boys (punish) _____ yesterday because of the damage they caused.

8. I (study—*progressive*) _____ for my examination now instead of reading the comics.

9. Why (they, punish) _____ the boy so severely yesterday?

10. I (look) _____ into this matter a long time ago.

11. His friends (help) _____ him when he was in trouble instead of criticizing him.

12. We (take) _____ more precautions against fire; if we had we would still have our house.

13. Henry (study) _____ last night, but he went to the movies instead.

14. My physician told me I (make) _____ an appointment[11] soon.

15. Traffic laws (obey) _____ by motorists and pedestrians.

B. Based on the sentence given below, tell what someone had better do *or* had better not do.

EXAMPLE: a. Jack has a bad cold.

He'd better stay in bed. (Note that the contraction for **had** is '**d**.)

b. It's raining very hard outside.

We'd better not go to the movies.

1. This melon isn't ripe yet.

_____

2. The phone is ringing.

_____

3. His shoes are worn out.

_____

4. Mary spilled some coffee on her dress.

_____

5. The point of this pencil isn't sharp any more.

_____

6. We've done enough work today.

_____

[11]Since **should** is already a past form, it is correct for sequence of tenses in the past. **Should have** would mean that the action did not occur. **Ought to** is also acceptable in sequence of tenses.

7. Lucy has a bad toothache.

_____

8. We've been driving all day.

_____

9. There's a storm approaching.

_____

10. We're running out of gas.

_____

4-9
POSSIBILITY
MAY, CAN

May is the usual auxiliary for possibility.

Present or future time	It may (*or* might) rain tonight. (*Might* expresses less certainty.)
Past time	He may (*or* might) have gone to the party last night.

Can is also common as an auxiliary expressing possibility.

Present or future time	Something can (*or* may) go wrong. *or* Something could (*or* might) go wrong.
Past time	Something could (*or* may, might) have gone wrong.

Note that **may have, might have, could have** are used only for *past possibility,* not for permission or ability.

Use the correct form of **may** or **can** for possibility. In some sentences only **may** expresses possibility, and in some sentences only the present or the past auxiliary is acceptable.

EXAMPLE: a. It looks as though it (snow) <u>may</u> (*or* <u>might</u>) <u>snow</u> soon.

b. I can't find my umbrella. I (leave) <u>may</u> (*or* <u>might, could</u>) <u>have left</u> it at the office.

c. If the heavy rains continue, they (damage) <u>may</u> (*or* <u>might, can, could</u>) <u>damage</u> the crops.

d. They (try) <u>may</u> (*or* <u>might, could</u>) <u>be trying</u> to phone us right now.

e. He (pass) <u>might</u> (*or* <u>could</u>) <u>have passed</u> the examination if he had studied harder.[12]

f. (The missing child, kidnap) <u>Could</u> (*or* <u>might</u>) <u>the missing child have been kidnapped</u> yesterday?

[12]In sentences with unreal conditions, only the past form of the auxiliary is used.

1. You (be) _____ right after all.

2. The jury (decide) _____ that he is really innocent even though there is much circumstantial evidence against him.

3. These products (purchase) _____ at any drug store.

4. What (cause) _____ the delay now?

5. (He, be) _____ at his home rather than at his office at this hour?

6. His plane (shoot down) _____ on his last flight over enemy territory.

7. They (have) _____ dinner right now.

8. John said he (be able) _____ to go on the trip, but he wasn't sure.

9. He (cheat) _____ at cards when he was shot by one of the players.

10. What would you do if you (do) _____ anything you wanted to?

11. You (interest) _____ in looking over this travel folder.

12. At this time he (look, *progressive*) _____ for an excuse not to do the job.

13. She (not be) _____ able to find her husband in that crowd.[13]

14. When they return to their home town, they (not find) _____ anyone they know.

15. We (not come) _____ if we had known you would not be there.

4-10
NECESSITY
MUST, HAVE TO

The difference between obligation and necessity is often one of degree only. Statements with **should** and **ought to** suggest a desirable course of action, which may or may not be acted on—*You should do your homework every day*. Statements with **must** and **have to** are stronger and do not include the possibility of choice—*You must do your homework every day*. **Must** is generally felt as stronger than **have to**.

In the sense of necessity, the past form for **must** is **had to**—**I had to meet my cousin yesterday.** This past form is required in the sequence of tenses. Thus, **He tells me I *must* do it** becomes **He told me I *had to* do it.**[14]

Have got to is an informal equivalent of **have to.** It has only a present form.

---

[13]Usually only **may** (*or* **might**) is used for negative possibility.
[14]In informal English, the present form **must** is often heard in sequence of tenses—
He told me I must do it.

Use the correct form of **must** or **have to.** Use both auxiliaries if they are possible.

EXAMPLE: a. I (leave) <u>must leave *or* have to leave</u> right away.

b. I (leave) <u>had to leave</u> the party early last night.

c. You (not sit) <u>mustn't sit</u> so close to the fire. (**Must not** is used for a prohibition or a warning.)

d. You (not pay) <u>don't have to pay</u> in person; you can pay by check. (**not have to** = not be required to)

e. (We write) <u>Must we write *or* Do we have to write</u> a thesis in order to get a degree? (Only the **do** auxiliary is used in questions and negatives with **have to.**)

1. I (go) _____ to the bank to make a deposit.

2. You (pay) _____ your rent at once or I will have you evicted.

3. We (eat) _____ in order to live.

4. He asked the teacher whether he (hand in) _____ his composition immediately even though he hadn't finished it.

5. He feels he (read) _____ every book on the subject before he can write his own book.

6. (You, make) _____ so much noise?

7. Students (not write) _____ their homework in pencil because it's hard to read.

8. You (not go) _____ home if you don't want to. You can stay here overnight.

9. I have often wondered whether he (do) _____ what he did.

10. You (not copy) _____ from others during an examination.

11. They (comply) _____ with the building code, or they will not be granted permission to build.[14]

12. All books (return) _____ by the end of the term.

13. Years ago people (read) _____ by candlelight.

14. (Everyone, go) _____ to the meeting tomorrow?

15. We (not be) _____ late for the meeting.

16. Students (attend) _____ all classes. However, they (not participate) _____ in extracurricular activities.

17. You (not touch) _____ that wire or you'll get an electric shock.

18. (You, leave) _____ so early?

[14]**Will** may be used with **have to.**

4-11
INFERENCE WITH *MUST*

Must is often used to make a guess about an event in the present or in the past.

> I hear the sound of fire engines. **There must be a fire nearby.** (Inference about the present.)

> Yesterday I went to a music festival. **There must have been 1,000 people in the audience.** (Inference about past time. **Must have** is used only for past inference, not past necessity.)

Tell what can be inferred from the following statements. Possibilities are suggested by the words in parentheses.

Inference about Present Time

EXAMPLE: a. I haven't seen her for a few days. (sick)
   She must be sick.

   b. There is a big furniture van in front of our neighbors' house. (moving)
   They must be moving.

   c. The boys are carrying sleeping bags. (go on a camping trip)
   They must be going on a camping trip.

1.   The cat has not been eating all day. (not feel well)

_____

2.   Look out the window. There's almost no one out in the street today. (very cold)

_____

3.   This milk is very thin and watery. (skim milk)

_____

4.   The students entering the classroom are carrying wet unbrellas. (rain)

_____

5.   He owns a boat and an airplane. (very rich)

_____

6.   The grandstand benches are being put out on the street. (get ready for a big parade)

_____

7.   Nobody answers the phone. (out to lunch)

_____

8.   The dentist will not take any new patients now. (very busy)

_____

9.   The door won't open. (not have the right key)

_____

10.   He was too busy to eat lunch. (very hungry now)

_____

11.   I've tried to call them several times today. (not be in town)

_____

Inference about Past Time

Example: a.   I can't find my watch anywhere. (lose)
                    <u>I must have lost it.</u>

              b.   The coffee tastes bitter. (boil too long)
                    <u>It must have been boiling too long.</u>

1.   I never received your letter. (lose in the mails)

_____

2.   When he walked into the classroom the students were busy writing. (take a test)

_____

3.   The ground is covered with snow. (snow last night)

_____

4.   The cake is burned on the edges. (be in the oven too long)

_____

5.   Her hair looks beautiful today. (go to the hairdresser's)

_____

6.   The children returned from the picnic tired but in good spirits. (have a good time)

_____

7.   Look at this picture of my grandmother. (be very beautiful when she was young)

_____

8.   The plane hasn't arrived yet. (delay because of the bad weather)

_____

9.   I can't find my wallet. (leave at home)

_____

10.   There's a mistake in my figures. (not add right)

_____

4-12
EXPECTATION, *SHOULD*

In addition to obligation or advisability, **should**—and to a lesser extent **ought to**—may indicate expectation.

Present or future	It's five o'clock. The train should (*or* ought to) be here any moment.
Past	I sent the package a week ago. It should (*or* ought to) have arrived by now. I don't know what's the matter. The train should have been here an hour ago. (*expectation not realized*)

A. In the following sentence, use should for expectation with reference to the present, or **should have** with reference to the past.

EXAMPLE: a. I <u>should finish</u> this letter by 10 o'clock.

b. We ordered the books months ago. They (arrive) <u>should have arrived</u> long before now.

1. The messenger is on his way. He (get) _____ to your office in a few minutes.

2. He (be back) _____ from his hunting trip any day now.

3. The doctor thinks the child (get—*progressive*) _____ better soon.

4. We don't understand what's delaying them. They (be) _____ here an hour ago.

5. Mr. Harris is busy now, but he (be) _____ able to see you in a few minutes.

6. My wife is preparing dinner now. It (be) _____ ready soon.

7. People are getting on the bus now. It (leave—*progressive*)

_____ in a few minutes.

8. I'm beginning to get worried. They (write) _____ us long before this.

9. It's a clear day. The stars (be) _____ very bright tonight.

10. Look in that cabinet. The files you want (be) _____ there.

11. The plane is just now landing. It (arrive) _____ hours ago.

12. The snow has stopped falling. We (be) _____ able to go out soon.

B. Go over the sentences in A using **ought to, ought to have** instead of **should, should have.**

EXAMPLE: a. I ought to finish this letter by 10 o'clock.

b. We ordered the books months ago. They ought to have arrived long before now.

C. Should for expectation is related to **must** for inference. Occasionally these auxiliaries are interchangeable, **must** merely expressing a greater degree of certainty.

We airmailed the letter a few days ago. It should (*or* must) be there now.

We airmailed the letter a few days ago. It should have (*or* must have) arrived by now.

However, while **should** may be used for future expectation (**It should arrive soon**), **must** cannot be used for future inference.

Use **should** or **should have** for expectation, or **must** or **must have** for inference. In some sentences, two choices are possible. Note whether the auxiliaries you use are for expectation, for inference, or both.

EXAMPLE: a. I don't see him anywhere. He (be) must be out for lunch. (*inference*)

b. The cake has been in the oven for 35 minutes. It (be) should *or* must be ready. (*expectation and inference*)

c. His credit card was mailed a week ago. He (receive) should *or* must have received it by now. (*expectation and inference*)

d. One of my classmates looks quite depressed. He (not pass) must not have passed the examination. (*inference*)

1. His temperature is going down. He (feel) _____ better soon.

   _____

2. I can't find my umbrella. I (leave) _____ it at the office.

   _____

3. What's keeping him? He (be) _____ here a long time ago.

   _____

4. The plane has been missing for a week. It (crash) _____ in the mountains during the storm. _____

5. The trip from the airport takes only a half hour. He (be) _____ here an hour ago. _____

6. He has extended his visit to Hawaii. He (enjoy—*progressive*) _____ the balmy breezes there.

   _____

7. The check has just been sent out. You (get) _____ it in a day or two. _____

8. They have never acknowledged receipt of my gift. They (not receive)
   _____ it. _____

9. The girl didn't answer when the teacher called on her. She (be)
   _____ daydreaming. _____

10. There's no heat today. Something (go) _____ wrong with the
    furnace. _____

11. Something is wrong. The heat (come up) _____ from the
    basement furnace an hour ago. _____

12. I can't get a dial tone on this telephone. It (be) _____ out of
    order. _____

13. He is smoking a strong cigar. He (not be) _____ aware that
    it is disturbing some of the guests. _____

14. The lunar spaceship is already in orbit around the earth. It (reach)
    _____ the moon in a few days.

    _____

15. I've just turned on the air conditioner. It (start) _____ to get
    cool here soon. _____

16. She's still working at her desk. She (not realize) _____ that
    it's time to leave. _____

17. She's typing the last page. It (not take) _____ her much
    longer to finish the letter. _____

18. It's 7:30. The play (start—*progressive*) _____ soon.

    _____

4-13
WOULD RATHER

Would rather,[15] which is a synonym for *prefer,* is often included among the auxiliaries. It has a present and a past form.

Present form *(now, or in general)*	**I would rather wear** a fur coat than a cloth coat in the winter.
Past form	**I would rather have worn** a fur coat than a cloth coat last winter.

---

[15]**Had rather** is an older variant of **would rather.**

Note the use of **than** before the second item. **Would rather** often involves a choice (sometimes implied) between two alternatives. **Would rather not** is the negative form.

A. Replace the sentences with prefer with sentences containing would rather plus the words in parentheses. Use than before the second choice. Do not use to after rather. (Write your answers on the lines marked A.)

EXAMPLE: a. She prefers   dancing   to   anything else.
                  (go dancing)   (do anything else)

   A. <u>She would rather go dancing than do anything else.</u>

   b. The Browns prefer   the movies   to   the theater.
                  (go to the movies)   (go to the theater)
   A. <u>The Browns would rather go to the movies than (go) to the theater.</u>

   (If the second verb is the same as the first, it is often omitted.)

1. We all prefer   peace   to   war.
          (have peace)   (be at war)

   A. _____

   B. _____

2. Mrs. Jones prefers   France   to   England.
          (live in France)   (live in England)

   A. _____

   B. _____

3. The children prefer   the porch   to   the bedroom.
          (sleep in the porch)   (sleep in the bedroom)

   A. _____

   B. _____

4. He prefers   the ocean   to   a lake.
          (swim in the ocean)   (swim in a lake)

   A. _____

   B. _____

5. They prefer staying at home to going out on New Year's Eve.
          (stay at home)   (go out on New Year's Eve)

   A. _____

   B. _____

6. They prefer eating at home to eating in a restaurant.
          (eat at home)   (eat in a restaurant)

   A. _____

   B. _____

7. I prefer not eating out at all to eating with unpleasant company.
        (not eat out at all)   (eat with unpleasant company)

    A. _____

    B. _____

B. Change the sentences in A using **would rather have** to express *past preference.* (Write your answers on the lines marked B.)

EXAMPLE: a. B. She would have rather have gone dancing than (have) done anything else.

            b. B. The Browns would rather have gone to the movies than (have gone) to the theater.

C. **Would rather** is sometimes confused with **had better**. What must be kept in mind is that **would rather** has the meaning of **preference**, and **had better** signifies **advisability**.

> It's getting late. We'd better leave the office now or we'll miss the last bus.
> (we'd better = it would be advisable for us to. The contraction **'d** for **had** is often used.)
> I'd rather take a taxi home than ruin my clothes in the rain.
> (I'd rather = I would prefer to. The contraction **'d** for **would** is often used.)

Both **would rather** and **had better** are made negative by placing **not** after them.

> I would rather not make such a big investment at this time.
> I had better not spend so much money now.

Use **had better, would rather, would rather have.** Remember that **had better** expresses advisability; **would rather** expresses preference, and it often requires **than** before the second choice. (For this exercise, do not use the contracted form.)

EXAMPLE: a. He (paint) <u>would rather paint</u> than do anything else.

            b. In the past, the elderly couple (travel) <u>would rather have traveled</u> than stayed at home.

            c. I think we (not take) <u>had better not take</u> a vacation this year because we don't have much money.

1. He told the police that he (go) _____ to prison than betray his friend.

2. Adam and Eve (stay) _____ in the Garden of Eden than been expelled from it.

3. The doctor told her she (sleep)[16] _____ on a hard mattress if she wanted to avoid backaches.

4. In the last war, the young children (go) _____ to school than sought shelter from bombs.

---

[16]Since **had better** and **would rather** include past forms, they may be used in sequence of tenses after a past verb.

5. We (take) _____ the clothes off the line before it starts to rain.

6. He (eat) _____ more sensibly if he doesn't want to get sick.

7. He (commute) _____ from the suburbs than live in the city.

8. I (do) _____ things for myself than ask other people to do them for me.

9. You (not waste) _____ so much time if you want to catch the train.

10. When he was a child, he (have) _____ love than material things.

11. I think you (see) _____ the doctor right away.

12. If I have a choice, I (not continue) _____ my studies at this school.

13. The hotel clerk asked the guests whether they (have)[16] _____ a room facing the mountains or the sea.

14. The children were told that they (not feed) _____ the animals in the zoo.

15. I (go) _____ to Europe by boat than by plane.

4-14
AUXILIARIES WITH *TO*

The modal auxiliaries with **to** that have already been given are **be able to** (= **can**), **ought to** (= **should**), and **have to** or informal **have got to** (= **must**). Other auxiliaries with **to** are:

1. **Used to**—meaning past custom

> He *used to play* tennis very often when he was young.
> negative—He *didn't use to play* tennis very often when he was young.
> question—*Did he use to play* tennis very often when he was young?

Other ways of expressing past custom are with the auxiliary **would** or with the simple past—**He would play** (*or* **played**) **tennis very often when he was young.**

2. **Be to**—meaning be required to, be supposed to, be scheduled to

> You were to do your homework in ink.
> The train is to leave tonight.

In the following sentences, change the auxiliaries to the synonomous forms with **to** (**be able to, ought to, have to** or informal **have got to**). Also, change **be required to, be supposed to, be scheduled to** to **be to.**

EXAMPLE: a. I *can* fix that for you right away.

> I will be able to fix that for you right away.

b. You *should* have taken care of that matter a long time ago.
   You ought to have taken care of that matter a long time ago.

c. I *must* pay this bill before the end of the month.
   I have to pay (informal I've got to pay) this bill before the end of the month.

d. *Must* you leave so soon?
   Do you have to leave so soon? *or* Have you got to leave so soon?

e. Even as a child, he *would* sit and write poetry for hours.
   Even as a child, he used to sit and write poetry for hours.

f. All the salesgirls *are required to* dress neatly.
   All the salesgirls are to dress neatly.

1. I *must* see him now.

_____

2. When he was young, he *would* go for a long walk every morning.

_____

3. You *are supposed to* hand in your assignments every day.

_____

4. *Must* these forms be filled out right away?

_____

5. Students *are required to* type their research papers.

_____

6. *Can* the doctor give me an appointment today?

_____

7. He *should* have worked for a living, instead of accepting his wife's money.

_____

8. The usher is telling him that he *must* be quiet in the movies.

_____

9. You *should* get more rest.

_____

10. When he went to high school, he *wouldn't* pay any attention to his teachers.

_____

11. She *couldn't* come to work because she was sick.

_____

12. *Is* everyone in the office *required to* work overtime tonight?

_____

13. Everyone *must* have food and shelter.

_____

14. She *should* be doing her housework instead of gossiping with her neighbor.

_____

15. When he lived at the beach, *would* he go swimming often?

_____

16. The announcement *was supposed to* have been made today, but so far we've heard nothing.

_____

17. She *shouldn't* have put the bananas in the refrigerator.

_____

18. The plane *is scheduled to* arrive at Kennedy Airport.

_____

4-15
USED TO vs *BE USED TO*

Used to past custom (no longer observed)	When I was a child, I *used to live* in the country.	**Used** is an auxiliary. **To** is the sign of the infinitive.
Be used to (mostly present custom)	Now I am *used to living* in the city.	**Be** is a full verb. **Used** is an adjective meaning **accustomed.** **To** is a preposition requiring the **-ing** form of the verb.

If progress toward acquiring a custom is to be expressed, **get** or **become** is used.

  Now I am even **getting** (or **becoming**) **used to** hearing all kinds of street noises.

Supply **used to** or a form of **be used to**. Use the simple form of the verb after **used to** and the **-ing** form of the verb after **be used to.**

EXAMPLE: a. A few years ago, an apartment in this town (cost) <u>used to cost</u> very little money.

  b. Now people in town (pay) <u>are used to paying</u> very high rent for an apartment.

1. My parents (travel) _____ to other countries when they were

  young, but now they (go) _____ to places that are nearby.

2. This street (be) _____ very dark until the new lights were installed.

3. He doesn't have any problem getting to work at 8:00 in the morning because he (get up) _____ early.

4. Once grandparents, parents, and children (live) _____ together, but now grandparents (live) _____ by themselves.

5. At one time American mothers (hope) _____ their sons would grow up to become President.

6. Before he became ill, he (play) _____ tennis every morning.

7. She's so (go to bed) _____ early that she hardly ever goes out at night.

8. For a long time, people (think) _____ that the world was flat and that people could fall off the edge.

9. They (have) _____ a lot of money, but now they are poor.

10. Today many children (watch) _____ TV for hours instead of doing their homework.

11. We (go) _____ to the country every summer, but now we can't afford to.

12. This street (be) _____ very quiet, but lately it has become quite noisy because of the heavy traffic.

13. I'm now (eat) _____ hamburgers, but at first I didn't like them.

14. In many banks, machines are doing the work that tellers (do) _____ .

15. People (catch) _____ fish in this river, but now the river has become polluted.

4-16
PAST AUXILIARIES
IN SEQUENCE OF TENSES

A past main verb often requires the past tense of the verb in a dependent clause.

Present	He *is giving* a check to the boy who *delivers* the newspapers.
Past	He *gave* a check to the boy who *delivered* the newspapers.

An auxiliary used with the verb in the dependent clause is in past form.

Present   **I'm** sure that he **will regret** his rude remarks.

Past   **I was** sure that he **would regret** his rude remarks.

Change each sentence to past time. Be sure to use the past form of the auxiliary in the dependent clause. (Some dependent clauses have more than one verb that need to be changed.)

EXAMPLE: a. She is planting the seeds which have been given to her by a friend.
     She *planted* the seeds which *had been given* to her by a friend.
     (Note that for a single action, the simple past tense may correspond to the present progressive tense.)

     b. He tells us that he cannot come because he is ill.
     He *told* us he *could not come* because he *was* ill. (two verbs in the dependent clause)

     c. Even though he can't afford it, he is buying a new home.
     Even though he *couldn't afford* it, he *bought* a new house.

1. I don't know who will do the job.

     _____

     _____

2. The police believe that the child may have been kidnapped.

     _____

     _____

3. The company wants to hire someone who can type well.

     _____

     _____

4. They agree that no more can be done than has been done already.

     _____

     _____

5. We wonder why they must always come late.

     _____

     _____

6. He is paying the boy who has been delivering the newspapers.

     _____

     _____

7. It is evident that he has been doing his best.

     _____

     _____

8.   Because the job can't be finished on schedule, they are asking for an extension of time.

_____

_____

9.   Although he should be writing some letters, he is watching television instead.

_____

_____

10.   We believe they must be out of town. (**Must** is used here for inference.)

_____

_____

11.   There is enough room on the ship only for those who must leave the country.

_____

_____

4-17
CONTRACTIONS WITH AUXILIARIES

Informally, an auxiliary may contract not only with the negative **not** that follows it, but with a word that precedes it. Contractions with **not** have already been taken up in the preceding chapter under negatives and questions. Such contractions take the following form:

Be		Have		Shall–will	
am	— 'm	has	— 's	shall–will	— 'll
is	— 's	have	— 've	should–would	— 'd
are	— 're	had	— 'd		

Note that **'s** is a contraction for **is** and **has**; **'d** is a contraction for **had** and **should** or **would**. The context makes clear which auxiliary is being contracted.

The auxiliary **do** and modal auxiliaries do not contract with the subject.

Contractions occur most often with pronouns, but they are also used with nouns and with introductory adverbs.

noun subject	The bus'll be here soon.
introductory adverb	How's he going to pay for all that?
	Here's the money I owe you.

A. Contractions with Words before Auxiliaries

Wherever possible, use a contraction with the auxiliary and the word before it.

1.   She is leaving on Saturday.

_____

2.   What have you got there?

_____

3.   They were stopped at the border.

_____

4.   Please see who is at the door.[17]

_____

5.   Who has the starring role in that movie?[17]

_____

6.   I had hoped to get here earlier, but my train was delayed.

_____

7.   She was late to work this morning.

_____

8.   Whom did they choose?

_____

9.   It is raining very hard now.

_____

10.   I am not eager to finish school quickly.

_____

11.   How will you pay for that car?

_____

12.   The paper has finally arrived.

_____

13.   I should like to hear from you.

_____

14.   You should be hearing from him soon.[18]

_____

15.   He would appreciate any help you can give him.

_____

[17]The independent verb **be** may contract with the subject, but not the independent verb **have.**
[18]No contraction occurs when **should** is the equivalent of the modal auxiliary **ought to.**

B. Contractions with Subjects or with NOT

Generally, except for the auxiliaries **am, is, are,** contractions with subjects are less likely than contractions with **not.**

Wherever possible, contract the auxiliary with both the subject and with **not.**

EXAMPLE: a. He is not planning to go to the party.
He's not planning to go to the party.
He isn't planning to go to the party.

b. I am not going to see him.
I'm not going to see him.[19]

1. They are not impressed by his record.

_____

_____

2. We were not allowed to enter the hospital room.

_____

_____

3. The girl was not in a hurry to leave.

_____

_____

4. The train has not arrived yet.[20]

_____

_____

5. The children have not eaten dinner yet.[20]

_____

_____

6. He will not permit this to happen again.

_____

_____

7. They would not enjoy that movie.

_____

_____

[19]**Ain't** is a grammatically incorrect contraction for **am not.**
[20]Contractions between noun subjects and auxiliaries represent very informal usage.

8. We cannot deny that he is charming.

_____

_____

9. He might not find the street without a map.

_____

_____

10. You must not say such things.

_____

_____

11. It is not difficult to do that.

_____

_____

4-18
DO AS AUXILIARY

The **do** auxiliary is accompanied by the simple form of the verb. It is used only in the *simple present* tense (**do** or **does offer**) and in the *simple past* tense (**did offer**).

Questions and Short Answers	**Do** you like my new hat? Yes, I do.
Negative Statements	I **don't** like your new hat.
Abridgement—omission or substitution	I don't like coffee and neither **does** my wife. Mary works harder than her sister **does**.
Emphasis	My teacher thinks I didn't study for my test, but I **did** study. The letter we were expecting never **did** arrive.

Supply **do, does,** *or* **did.**

1. How much _____ these shoes cost?

2. What _____ you buy yesterday?

3. Where _____ he go last night?

4. Why _____ you think he won't come tonight?

5. What _____ this word mean?

6. I _____ n't get any sleep at all last night.

7. He never _____ get to the station last night.

8. I _____ n't remember what his name is.

9. She _____ n't want his help now.

10. We _____ n't get your letter in time to meet you at the airport.

11. We often serve dinner outdoors, and so _____ our neighbors.

12. He likes to watch soccer on television, but his wife _____ n't.

13. The owner of the factory worked just as hard as his employees _____ in order to get the order out on time.

14. Although I have little time for entertainment, I _____ go to the theater once in a while.

15. He _____ have money, but it's all tied up in property.

16. How long _____ it generally take to fly from the East Coast to the West Coast?

17. They never go to bed before midnight and neither _____ their children.

18. She claims she can't cook, but she really _____ know how.

19. Everyone in the office worked late, and I _____ too.

REVIEW OF AUXILIARIES

Use the required auxiliary with each verb. In some sentences there are two or three possibilities. State whether the auxiliary expresses ability (**can, be able to**), permission (**may, can**), obligation or advisability (**should, ought to, had better**), possibility (**may**), necessity (**must, have to**), inference (**must**), expectation (**should**), preference (**would rather**), past custom (**used to**), futurity (**will**), or unreal condition (**would, might**).

EXAMPLE: a. My friend always wears very expensive dresses to school. Her parents (have) <u>must have</u> a lot of money. (*inference*)

b. I (take) <u>should take</u> better care of my garden, but I don't have enough time. (obligation, advisability)

c. He said there was a possibility that the concert (call off) <u>might</u> (*or* <u>would</u>) <u>be called off</u> (*possibility, futurity*).

d. My cold is getting worse. I (stay) <u>had better</u> (*or* <u>should</u>) <u>stay</u> home today. (*advisability*)

1. We (get) _____ to the airport by nine o'clock; otherwise we'll miss our plane. _____

2. When I was a youngster, I (not worry) _____ about anything at all. _____

3. No one (live) _____ without food.

   _____

4. I (prepare) _____ my income tax return last month, but I kept putting it off. Now I (do) _____ it if I don't want to pay a penalty for filing late. _____

5. (I help) _____ you clear the table?

   _____

6. His secretary asked whether she (have) _____ the afternoon off to do some shopping. _____

7. There is no more paper left, so I (not continue) _____ typing. _____

8. Any one of the three suspects (commit) _____ the murder yesterday. _____

9. He (be) _____ thankful that he wasn't hurt in that accident instead of complaining about the damage to his car. _____

10. He was warned that he (pay) _____ the fine or that he (put) _____ in prison. _____

11. This wine is excellent. You (try) _____ it.[21]

    _____

12. He (eat) _____ less if he wants to lose weight.

    _____

13. I (see) _____ you at once. I have important news for you.

    _____

14. You (not listen) _____ to him. He will only cause you trouble. _____

15. I (pay) _____ this bill immediately or I will be charged additional interest. _____

16. All the necessary documents (file) _____ within the next week. _____

17. The authorities are trying to determine what (cause) _____ the plane crash. _____

---

[21]*Should,* or the stronger *must,* may be used for a recommendation.

18. We're almost out of bread. We (buy) _____ some more right away. _____

19. The doctor said that the patient (need) _____ an operation if his condition got any worse. _____

20. I don't know what the trouble is. They (be) _____ here long before now. _____

21. You (not make) _____ such sarcastic remarks to him when you saw him yesterday. _____

22. He (be) _____ very hungry now because he has had nothing to eat all day. _____

23. He (recover) _____ from his illness if he had really wanted to live. _____

24. They (decide) _____ not to come to the party; otherwise they (already be) _____ here.

    _____

25. It's not raining so hard now. It (clear up) _____ in a little while. _____

26. Most people (work) _____ during the day than at night.

    _____

27. This soup is very hot. You (not drink) _____ it until it cools off. _____

28. They (live) _____ in the country when they were children, but now they live in the city. _____

5

Adjectives

STRUCTURAL DESCRIPTION OF ADJECTIVES

Function	Form	Markers
Modifies a noun **beautiful** *girls*	Grammatical endings for comparison *-er, -est*	For comparison *more, most*
Modifies a pronoun *They are **beautiful**;* *something **new***	Derivational endings *-ous, -ic(al), -al,* *-ant* or *-ent, -ible* or *-able, -ful, -less,* *-y, -ish, -some,* etc.	intensifiers of degree *very, so, quite,* *too,* etc.

Position

1. Before a Noun

Determiners		Descriptive Adjectives			Noun Adjuncts
articles *a, the*	numerals *first three* *last ten,* etc.	general description *beautiful,* *intelligent,* *clear,* etc.	physical state size—*large* shape—*oval* age—*old* temperature— *cold* color—*red*	proper adjective nationality— *Irish* religion— *Catholic*	*college* (student) *gasoline* (station)
demonstratives *this, that*					
possessives *my, your*					
adjectives of indefinite quantity *some, much,* etc.					

2. After a Verb
a. after linking verbs (*be, seem, appear, look, become*)
   *She is **beautiful**.*
b. in objective complement position (after *make, consider, keep*)
   *His behavior made me **uneasy**.*

Determiners may be broken up into three groups—pre-determiners, the determiners themselves, and the post-determiners. All of these may be preceded by intensifiers of the entire noun phrase.[1]

Intensifiers (adverbs)	**Pre-determiners**	**Determiners**	**Post-determiners** (numbers)		
1	2	3	4		
even only just	both[2] all[2] half[2]	the, a this, that my, John's etc.	*Ordinal* *4a* first second third etc.	*Cardinal* *4b* one two three etc.	*4bb* other more
	Multipliers twice double triple many times ten times etc.	*Indefinite Adjectives* *3a* several some any either every each much many (a) few (a) little (the) less (the) least (the) most	*Sequence Adjectives* *4c* last next following	*4cc* few	

Note at column 3 header also: *3b* other / more

Note that **other** and **more** may be used not only after other indefinite adjectives (**several other people, many more books**), but after cardinal numbers (**three other people, two more books**).

Few follows **the first, the last, the next** (**the first few years, the next few days**).

---

[1]A noun phrase is the noun head with its preceding and following modification.
[2]**Both, all, half** may also be followed by **of**—**both (of) his children**.

Arrange the determiners in the proper order.

1. (the, both) girls were sent to camp.

   _____

2. (two, only, more) napkins are needed.

   _____

3. (first, Mary's, two) English teachers were very good.

   _____

4. The children were placed in (other, every) seat for the examination.

   _____

5. (two, first, the) men refused; (the, other, two)[3] men said they would consider the offer.

   _____

6. In (few, a, more) days we will be leaving for California.

   _____

7. He claims he needs (more, some) money; however, he has (much, more) money than he will admit.

   _____

8. (triple, the, even) appropriations granted last year will not be sufficient now.

   _____

9. (last, these, few) days have been very busy ones.

   _____

10. (the, half, only) concert hall was filled.[4]

   _____

11. (more, many) people came than were expected.

   _____

12. I have (half, just, a)[5] tank of gasoline left.

   _____

[3]**Other** may precede or follow a cardinal numeral.
[4]**Only** is an intensifier of the entire noun phrase. In the sense of *one,* **only** may appear after **the**—**the** *only* **other person in the room; the** *only* **way to do it.**
[5]**Half a** or **a half** may be used.

SEQUENCE OF ADJECTIVES BEFORE NOUNS

Determiners 1	Descriptive Adjectives 2			Noun Adjuncts 3	Nouns
	General Description	Physical State	Proper Adjective		
		(size, shape, age, temperature, color)	*(nationality, religion, etc.)* *(also some adjectives ending in -ic(al), -al, etc.)*		
both the a those three Jane's a that	air-conditioned beautiful, exclusive self-conscious daringly-cut temperamental	white little old very large	Lincoln Continental residential Parisian Buddhist Italian	evening opera	cars district ladies gown temple singer

Adjectives of general description or physical state may be modified by adverbs. These adverbs go directly before the adjectives they refer to (**very** large, **extremely** beautiful).

Commas generally appear only between two or more adjectives of general description. Commas between adjectives of general description and physical state are often optional.

The position of adjectives of general description and of physical state may sometimes be reversed.

Rewrite the following, arranging the words in parentheses in the proper order. Use commas where necessary.

1. (angry, those, young, all) men

_____

2. (very lively, black and white, a, little) kitten

_____

3. (muddy, steep, a, river) bank

_____

4. (bone, white, exquisitely designed) china

_____

5. (recent, stormy, wet, this) weather

_____

6. (ivory, little, intricately carved) figurines

_____

7. (sympathetic, that, young, English) teacher

_____

8. (white, expensive, Steinway, the teacher's) piano

_____

9. (gifted, young, college, black) students

_____

10. (old, American, two, colonial, spacious) houses

_____

11. (commercial, the, first, jet, ten) planes

_____

12. (small, very spoiled, two, French, black) poodles

_____

5-3
PROPER ADJECTIVES
ADJECTIVES OF NATIONALITY

Proper nouns and adjectives refer to nationalities, geographical places, religions, holidays, dates, names of people or organizations, titles, etc. Such words always begin with capital letters.

Proper Noun	Proper Adjective
Italy	**Italian** food
Paris	**Parisian** styles
Christianity	**Christian** beliefs
Arab	**Arabian** nights

Give the adjective used for each country. Then give the noun for a person coming from that country. Be sure to begin each word of nationality with a capital letter.

Germany   a ___German___ custom   He is a ___German___.

Japan   a ___Japanese___ custom   He is a ___Japanese___.

Ireland	an __Irish__ custom	He is an __Irishman__[6]	
Egypt	an _____ custom	He is an _____.	
Poland	a _____ custom	He is a _____.	
India	an _____ custom	He is an _____.	
Switzerland	a _____ custom	He is a _____.	
Holland	a _____ custom	He is a _____.	
Russia	a _____ custom	He is a _____.	
France	a _____ custom	He is a[6] _____.	
Canada	a _____ custom	He is a _____.	
Israel	an _____ custom	He is an _____.	
Spain	a _____ custom	He is a _____.	
Venezuela	a _____ custom	He is a _____.	
Turkey	a _____ custom	He is a _____.	
the United States	an _____ custom	He is an _____.	
Australia	an _____ custom	He is an _____.	
Hungary	a _____ custom	He is a _____.	
Greece	a _____ custom	He is a _____.	
Sweden	a _____ custom	He is a _____.	

5-4
COMPARISON OF ADJECTIVES

Adjectives are compared for three degrees: Positive (for two units in equal degree; comparative (for two units in unequal degree); and superlative (for three or more units).

In the positive degree, **as . . . as** makes the comparison.

She's **as** beautiful as her sister (is).

She's not **as** (or **so**) hard-working as her sister (is).

[6]For words of nationality ending in **-man,** there are some corresponding forms ending in **-woman,** for example, Frenchwoman, Englishwoman. However, only some dictionaries give Irishwoman, none give Dutchwoman.

The forms for the comparative and the superlative are as follows.

Comparative	-er _____ than	more _____ than
Superlative	the _____ -est	the most _____
	1. *adjectives with one syllable:* **taller than, the tallest** 2. adjectives with two syllables ending in: -y **dirtier than, the dirtiest** -le **nobler than, the noblest**	1. *adjectives with three or more syllables:* **more beautiful than. the most beautiful** 2. two syllable adjectives with derivational endings (-ful, -less, -ish, -ous, -ing, -ed, etc.): **more useful than, the most useful**

There are two-syllable adjectives with either form:
1. adjectives ending in **-er—clever, tender, bitter**
2. adjectives ending in **-ow—narrow, shallow, mellow**
3. adjectives ending in **-some—handsome, wholesome, lonesome** (the *-er, -est* endings are less formal)
4. others—**polite, profound, sincere, common, pleasant, cruel, quiet, stupid** (the *-er, -est* endings are less formal)

Irregular Comparison:

1. Positive	2. Comparative	3. Superlative
good	**better**	**best**
bad	**worse**	**worst**
far	**farther** (for distance—formal) **further** (for addition)	**farthest** **furthest**
little	**less**	**least**
much **many**	**more**	**most**

In adding **-er** or **-est** for comparison, keep in mind that:

1. Final *y* preceded by a consonant is changed to *i*—**livelier, tastier, luckier.**
2. A final single consonant preceded by a single vowel is doubled—**bigger, thinner, hottest.**
3. Final *e* is dropped—**simpler, largest, wider.**

A comparison may be made stronger by using **much** or **far** before the comparative; or by **far** before the superlative adjective.

They are **much** (*or* **far**) happier now than they have ever been.

She is **by far** the best doctor in town. (**By far** may also appear in final position)

Supply the comparative or superlative form of the adjective. Be sure to use **than** after the comparative and **the** before the superlative.

EXAMPLE: a. He is (greedy) <u>the greediest</u> man I have ever met.

b. The weather in Florida is (hot) <u>hotter than</u> the weather in my native country.

1. It is (good) _____ to give _____ to receive.

2. She is (helpless) _____ person I have ever known.

3. They are looking for a (big) _____ apartment _____ the one they now have.

4. He is by far (bad) _____ student in his class.

5. Some people are (reliable) _____ others.

6. He is much (familiar) _____ with modern painting _____ with modern music.

7. (Difficult) _____ job of all still remains to be done.

8. His works are far (creative) _____ those of his contemporaries.

9. (Hot) _____ months of the year in the United States are July and August.

10. She earns much (little) _____ money _____ her husband does.

11. If he ever gets out of his country he will try to live in (free) _____ country in the world.

12. The recipes in my cookbook are (simple) _____ the ones in your cookbook.

13. This library has far (many) _____ books _____ any library I have ever been in.

14. There is a belief that professors are absent-minded, but I have known some people who are much (absent-minded) _____ any professors.

15. This fan is (noisy) _____ the one we had before.

16. She is (thin) _____ the last time I saw her.

17. The lobby of this hotel is much (dirty) _____ and (shabby)

_____ it used to be.

5-5
DERIVATION (1)
ADDING ADJECTIVE SUFFIXES TO WORDS THAT END IN SILENT *E*

		Exceptions
Keep the **e** *before a consonant*	careful hopeless lively	awful
Drop the e before a vowel (*including y*)	desirable nervous practical observant noisy	*after* **c** *or* **g** noticeable, manageable (*to keep the sound* *"soft" before, a, o, u*)

Add the adjective suffixes to the words given below. Rewrite the words.

lone + ly _____

admire + able _____

use + less _____

excuse + able _____

noise + y _____

hygiene + ic _____

value + able _____

change + able _____

juice + y _____

courage + ous _____

notice + able _____

life + less _____

observe + ant _____

shame + ful _____

imagine + ary _____

outrage + ous _____

hypocrite + ical _____

waste + ful _____

awe + ful _____

replace + able _____

love + able[7] _____

grace + ious _____

[7]A few **-able** adjectives derived from one-syllable verbs may be spelled with or without the *e*—**us(e)able, lik(e)able, lov(e)able, sal(e)able**. The spelling with *e* is less common.

Final *y* becomes *i* before an added consonant or vowel.

> colony + al = colonial
> mercy + ful = merciful
> Exception: **y** preceded by a vowel—**boyish, joyous**

Add the adjective suffixes to the words given below. Rewrite the words.

mystery + ous _____	day + ly _____
mercy + less _____	beauty + ful _____
rely + able _____	family + ar _____
envy + ous _____	pity + ful _____
colony + al _____	envy + able _____
industry + ous _____	plenty + ful _____
ceremony + al _____	victory + ous _____
vary + ous _____	enjoy + able _____
city + wide[8] _____	harmony + ous _____

			rót	t	en
one-syllable word					
two-three syllable word		re	grét	t	able
	un	con	tról	l	able
Exceptions: excéllent, transférable					

Note that: 1) the added adjective suffix *begins with a vowel;* 2) the syllable before the adjective suffix ends in a *single consonant preceded by a single vowel;* and 3) the syllable before the added adjective suffix is *stressed.*

The same rule applies if the adjective suffix -*y* is added (sunny, foggy).

[8]The **y** does not change before the endings **-wide** (countrywide) and **-like** (ladylike).

Use the appropriate adjective. Be careful of the spelling.

1. The pavement is very (slip) _____ because of last night's heavy rain.

2. Some of the newly rich are more (snob) _____ than those whose families have been wealthy for a long time.

3. His piano recital was truly an (unforget) _____ experience.

4. The day was so (fog) _____ that you couldn't see a thing in front of you.

5. That was a (regret) _____ incident. Please accept our apologies.

6. Student groups all over the world are becoming more (rebel)

   _____ against authority.

7. He wears clothes that are casual, almost slovenly; his trousers are always (bag)

   _____.

8. This wine is (excel) _____.

9. These passes are not (transfer) _____; they may be used only by the persons to whom they were issued.

10. All the strawberries in this box are (rot) _____.

11. I don't think that comedian was very (fun). _____.

12. She seems to prefer (man) _____ clothes to feminine ones.

13. After the heavy rains, the roads became so (mud) _____ that they couldn't be used.

5-8
DERIVATION (4)
ADJECTIVES FROM NOUNS, VERBS

Adjectives from Nouns
(-y, -ly, -(i)al, -ous, -ic(*al*),
-ish, -like, -ary, or *-ery, -ful, -less,*
-wide)

Give the adjective forms of the nouns in parentheses. Make whatever spelling changes are necessary.

1. The name Philadelphia stands for the "City of (Brother)

   _____ Love."

2. She has always behaved in a (duty) _____ way toward her parents.

3. There's a cold wind blowing; I feel very (chill) _____.

4. A Cadillac is so (cost) _____ that most people cannot afford one.

5. What is the (geography)[9] _____ location of Canada?

6. Some neurotic people become (hysteria) _____ over any little emotional disturbance.

7. His recent religious conversion has made him so (piety)

   _____ that he is forever praying and fasting.

8. Remarks that sound as though they come out of a book are (book)

   _____.

9. It was very (courage) _____ of him to risk his life trying to save a drowning child.

10. The damage to this painting is so extensive that the painting is almost (value)

    _____.

11. A portrait that looks almost like the original is very (life)

    _____.

Adjectives from Verbs
(-*ent* or -*ant*, -*able* or -*ible*, -*ive*, -*ed*, -*ing*, -*some*, -*ile*, -(*at*)*ory*, -*worthy*)

Give the adjective forms of the verbs in parentheses. Make whatever spelling changes are necessary.

1. He won't go away. He's very (persist) _____ about seeing you.

2. Excessive smoking and drinking are (destroy) _____ of one's health.

3. He was so (persuade) _____ that the committee all agreed to accept his proposal.

4. In a few states, first degree murder is (punish) _____ by death in the electric chair.

5. He is very (hesitate) _____ about taking such a long trip.

6. It soon became (appear) _____ that he was lying.

7. Don't throw that tire away. It's still (service) _____.

8. What is so (amaze) _____ is that no one was seriously hurt in that car accident.

[9]Some adjectives may end in either -**ic** or -**ical**—historic(al), philosophic(al).

9. Parents like their children to be (obey) _____.

10. I have walked too much; my ankles have become (swell)

    _____.

11. This material is (stain-resist) _____.

5-9
DERIVATION (5)

Supply the adjective forms that are required because of the preceding italicized words.

EXAMPLE: a. The dancer's *flexibility* of movement is remarkable. I never thought that a person could be so <u>flexible</u>.

b. He has great *sympathy* for his fellowmen. Such a <u>sympathetic</u> man is hard to find.

1. His parents *permit* him to do whatever he pleases. This

    _____ attitude is certainly going to spoil the child.

2. This registration form doesn't require an *explanation*. It is

    self-_____.

3. This house has a great deal of *space* to put things. We were lucky to find such a

    _____ house.

4. Those two men have been *quarreling* for some time. They are both very

    _____.

5. I hope I did not *offend* you. I would not like to be _____ to
    you in any way.

6. There is sometimes a great difference between *theory* (1) and *practice* (2).

    _____ (1) knowledge is often useless unless it can be applied

    in a _____ (2) way.

7. He does everything with great *enthusiasm* (1). No one can accuse him of *apathy* (2). A

    person who is _____ (1) gets much more work done than one

    who is _____ (2).

8. He spoke with great *force* (1) and *vigor* (2). But he could not *persuade* (3) the commit-

    tee, because an argument, besides being _____ (1) and

    _____ (2), can be _____ (3) only if
    it is backed by facts.

9. She always has a guilty *conscience* if she doesn't do things in a

    _____ way.

10. People who do things according to an orderly *system* are

    _____.

11. You've made a great *number* of mistakes on this report; they're too

    _____ to be overlooked.

5-10
***-ING*, *-ED*, ADJECTIVES (1)**

The present participle ending in **-ing,** and the past participle ending in **-ed** for regular verbs[10] are often used as adjectives.

A. Use the -ing, -ed participial adjectives as in the example.

EXAMPLE: *The game excited the audience.*

The game was <u>exciting</u>   The audience was <u>excited</u>
The <u>exciting</u> game   The <u>excited</u> audience
(*active* force—the **-ing** adjective goes with the   (*passive* force—the **-ed** adjective goes with the
original *subject* of a sentence)   original *object* of a sentence)

1. *The work tired the boy.*

The work was _____   The boy was _____

The _____ work   The _____ boy

2. *The lecture stimulated the students.*

The lecture was _____   The students were _____

The _____ lecture   The _____ students

3. *The experience disappointed the men.*

The experience was _____   The men were _____

The _____ experience   The _____ men

4. *The teacher's display of anger astonished the children.*

The teacher's display of anger was _____   The children were _____

The teacher's _____ display of anger   The _____ children

5. *The sight of a bear nearby terrified the campers.*

The sight of a bear nearby was _____   The campers were _____

The _____ sight of a bear nearby   The _____ campers

[10]For irregular verbs, the past participle is the *third* principal part (tear, tore, **torn**)

6. *The chemical substance purified the water.*

The chemical substance was _____   The water was _____

The _____ chemical substance   The _____ water.

5-11
-*ING*, -*ED*, ADJECTIVES (2)

B. Supply the correct participial adjective. Keep in mind that the **-ing** participle goes with an original *subject* and has *active* force; the **-ed** participle goes with an original *object* and has *passive* force.

EXAMPLE: a.   That was the most (thrill) <u>thrilling</u> experience I have ever had. (The experience was thrilling.)

b.   The (defeat) <u>defeated</u> army laid down their arms. (The army was defeated.)

1.   The young writer was pleased with the editor's (encourage)

_____ remarks.

2.   Such an experiment is valid only under rigidly (control)

_____ conditions.

3.   The (attack) _____ forces laid siege to the city for a long time.

4.   The (shock) _____ news of her son's death caused her to sob uncontrollably.

5.   She is a very (fascinate) _____ woman.

6.   The (disgust) _____ critic left the theater long before the end of the play.

7.   He made a (surprise) _____ financial recovery after his bankruptcy.

8.   His disease is already in a very (advance) _____ state.

9.   The Salvation Army collects (discard) _____ clothes and household goods.

10.   Spices and herbs act as (flavor) _____ agents.

11.   The (wash) _____ and (iron)

_____ clothes should be put in this drawer.

12.   She is throwing out all her (tear) _____ or (stain)

_____ linen.

13.   The pictures will be taken by a (hide) _____ camera.

14.   A (break) _____ spring caused all the trouble.

15. To see a (love) _____ parent and a (smile)

_____ baby is a (reward) _____ experience.

16. He drove a (rent) _____ car to the (desert)

_____ house, but the (lock) _____ door prevented him from getting in.

17. Ice cream and sherbet are (freeze) _____ desserts.

18. In this (change)[11] _____ world, new technologies are constantly being developed.

5-12
MUCH–MANY, (A) LITTLE (A) FEW, LESS–FEWER

In English, adjectives do not change their form when used with plural nouns—an intelligent man, some intelligent plans. One exception involves the demonstrative adjectives: **this**—singular, **these**—plural; **that**—singular, **those**—plural. Another exception involves the use of different adjectives for a noncountable noun and a plural countable noun.

Noncountable Nouns	Plural Countable Noun
Much furniture **is** needed.	**Many** chairs **are** needed.
(A) **Little** furniture **is** needed.	(A) **Few** chairs **are** needed.
Less furniture **is** needed.	**Fewer**[12] chairs **are** needed.

A little, a few stress the *presence* of something in a small quantity (**I have a little money; I have a few friends**); **little, few** stress the *absence* of almost all quantity (**I have little money; I have few friends**).

A lot of, or lots of are informal equivalents of either **much** or **many.**

> He has a lot of (= much) money.
>
> There are a lot of (= many) people on the train.

Underline the correct forms.

EXAMPLE: a. There (was, <u>were</u>) (much, <u>many</u>) accidents on the wet road.

b. (<u>Much</u>, many) more information (<u>is</u>, are) necessary before we can write up the report. (**Much or many** may function as an intensifier of **more.**)

---

[11]With some words, the **-ing** form represents action in progress (the increasing rate of exchange), while the **-ed** form represents a state or condition which has already come into existence. (the increased rate of exchange).

[12]In informal speech **less** is also used with plural nouns—**less chairs.**

1. There is (much, many) more beautiful scenery in the mountains than in the plains.

2. (Little, a little) soap (is, are) all we will need.

3. (Much, many) students (was, were) hurt in the riot.

4. I still have (little, a little) money left, enough to go to the movies.

5. (Much, many) more electrical appliances (is, are) being used in the home now than (was, were) used only a decade ago.

6. Only (a few, few) trees (was, were) damaged in the storm.

7. There (is, are) too (much, many) baggage in the luggage compartment of the train.

8. (Fewer, less) children (get, gets) polio today than in the past.

9. (Much, many) news (is, are) being broadcast over the radio and on television.

10. How (much, many) clothing are you taking for your trip?

11. There (is, are) (much, many) advertising in American newspapers.

12. Educated people use (little, few) slang.

13. How (much, many) machines (is, are) in operation now?

14. (Much, many) expensive machinery (is, are) required to do the job.

15. You have made too (much, many) mistakes on this paper.

16. There (was, were) very (much, many) people on the excursion boat.

17. So (much, many) equipment (was, were) purchased for the factory that the company had (little, a little) money left to furnish the office.

18. Even late at night you can find (few, a few) people still working at their desks.

19. (Few, a few) people (have, has) ever entered his home.

20. How (much, many) slices of toast would you like?

5-13
ADJECTIVES USED
IN THE COMPARISON OF NOUNS

Mary's hat	is	like similar to the same as	Jane's (hat).

or

Mary's hat	and	Jane's (hat)	are	alike. similar. the same.

The same may also immediately precede the noun—Mary is wearing the same hat as/Jane.

Like and similar imply that there may be some small differences between the items compared; the same implies that there is no difference.

Supply the proper adjectives for the comparisons of nouns made in the following sentences. Use the same number of words as there are blanks. Be sure to use **the** before **same.**

EXAMPLE: a. Your car is <u>the same as</u> mine. The two cars are <u>the same</u>.

b. The coat you just bought is <u>like</u> the one I bought last year. The two coats are <u>alike</u>.

1. His income and that of his wife are _____

   _____. His income is _____

   _____ _____ that of his wife.

2. He told a story _____ the one his father did. The two stories

   were very much _____.

3. Our house is just _____ our neighbor's. The two houses are

   _____.

4. The styles today are _____ _____
   the styles worn some time ago.

5. It doesn't matter which typewriter you use. They're both

   _____.

6. The suit he's wearing now is _____

   _____ the one I'm wearing. The two suits are

   _____.

7. They both do _____ _____ kind
   of work.

8. This lake is _____ _____ the lake
   I used to swim in when I was a child. The two lakes are

   _____.

9. Vegetables from the store are not _____

   _____ _____ vegetables from the

   garden.

Review of Adjectives

A. Rewrite the following, arranging the words in parentheses in the proper order. Use commas where necessary.

1. (the, both) girls _____

2. (muddy, steep, a, river) bank _____

3. (first, Mary's, two, English) teachers _____

4. (the, half, only) concert hall _____

5. (white, expensive, Steinway, the teacher's) piano _____

6. (small, very spoiled, two, French, black) poodles _____

B. Give the adjective form of the following words. Be careful of the spelling.

courage _____   rely _____

rebel _____   number _____

hysteria _____   appear _____

excel _____   conscience _____

obey _____   system _____

swell _____   sympathy _____

France _____   quarrel _____

Holland _____   cost _____

notice _____   offend _____

vary _____   destroy _____

slip _____   enthusiasm _____

mystery _____   persuade _____

C. Supply the comparative or superlative form of the adjective, together with any other required words. Be careful of the spelling.

1. It is (good) _____ to give _____ to receive.

2. They are looking for a (big) _____ apartment _____ the one they now have.

3. He is by far (bad) _____ student in his class.

4. (difficult) _____ job of all still remains to be done.

5. She earns much (little) _____ money

_____ her husband does.

6. This library has far (many) _____ books

_____ any library I have ever been in.

D. Supply the -ing present participle or the -ed past participle adjectives. (Some of the past participle adjectives may be irregular.)

1. The young writer was pleased with the editor's (encourage)

_____ remarks.

2. Such an experiment is valid only under rigidly (control)

_____ conditions.

3. The Salvation Army collects (discard) _____ clothes and house-hold goods.

4. She is throwing out all her (tear) _____ or (stain)

_____ linen.

5. Ice cream and sherbet are (freeze) _____ desserts.

E. Underline the correct forms.

1. (Little, a little) soap (is, are) all we will need.

2. There (is, are) too (much, many) baggage in the luggage compartment of the train.

3. (Much, many) news (is, are) being broadcast over the radio and on television.

4. Educated people use (little, few) slang.

5. You have made too (much, many) mistakes on this paper.

6. Even late at night you can find (few, a few) people still working at their desks.

7. How (much, many) slices of toast would you like?

6

Articles

The (Definite Article)	**A** (Indefinite Article)
Developed from a word meaning **this**. Signals a *particular* person or thing—*the student sitting next to you*. Used with singular or plural nouns.	Developed from a word meaning **one**. **An** used before vowel sounds. Signals an *unspecified* one of others—*a student sitting in the front row*. Used chiefly with singular countable nouns.

<table>
<tr><td>

Uses

1. For known persons or objects in the environment
   *He walked into **the** house and hung his coat in **the** closet.*
2. For persons, things, or ideas particularized by the verbal context
   a. preceding context—***A** strange dog came onto **the** porch. **The** dog seemed very friendly.*
   b. following context—***The** man **standing near the window** will be our guest speaker tonight.*
3. For a class as a whole
   ***The** lion is an animal.*
4. With a "ranking" adjective
   ***the** best way; **the** fifth lesson*
5. With nouns or gerunds + **of** phrases
   ***the** election of officers*
   ***the** changing of the guards*
6. In **of** phrases after words of quantity
   *most of **the** men in the factory*
   *four of **the** children from that school*
7. For place names
   ***the** Mississippi River*
   ***the** Alps*

</td><td>

Uses

1. In the sense of *one*, or *each*
   *I waited **an** hour.*
   *His rent is $200 **a** month.*
2. For an unidentified member of a class
   *We saw **a** lion at the zoo.*
3. For a representative member of a class
   a. identifying an individual member
      *That animal is **a** lion.*
   b. defining a smaller class
      *The lion is **an** animal.*

</td></tr>
</table>

6-1
A vs. *AN*

An is used before a word beginning with a vowel *sound*.

> an apple, an accident
> an hour, but a horrible event
> a university, but an unusual event

Use **a** or **an** before the following words.

_____ argument	_____ European journalist
_____ unavoidable delay	_____ garage
_____ half hour	_____ holiday
_____ union	_____ umbrella
_____ heiress	_____ hourly application
_____ humiliating experience	_____ useful gadget
_____ herb	_____ honest man
_____ ugly child	_____ yellow dress
_____ unique opportunity	_____ humid day
_____ uninvited guest	_____ unanimous decision
_____ universal feeling	_____ huge tree
_____ historical occasion	_____ humorous story
_____ underdeveloped country	_____ hospital
_____ human being	_____ honorable person

6-2
ARTICLE vs. NO ARTICLE (1)

The most important rule about the use of articles is that *an article is required with a singular countable noun*.

> I need _____ furniture (noncountable noun)[1]
> I need _____ chairs (plural countable noun)
> I need __the *or* a_____ chair (singular countable noun)

[1]See Exercise 1-5, pp. 6–8 for noncountable nouns.

The article is required even if a descriptive adjective accompanies the singular countable noun.

I need a comfortable chair.

However, if a determiner other than the article accompanies the noun, the article is not used.

I need this (or my, another, one) chair.

Supply the article **a** if it is required.

EXAMPLE: a. He requested <u>a</u> prompt reply to his letter.

b. He deserves __ admiration for his work.

c. There will be <u>a</u> brief pause for intermission.

1. She likes to eat _____ good food.

2. He made _____ bad mistake in his report.

3. He has accumulated _____ great wealth from his investments.

4. He is consulting with _____ authority on urban development.

5. She wants to become _____ nurse.

6. They asked him _____ difficult question.

7. _____ honesty and _____ loyalty are rare virtues.

8. They celebrated their victory with _____ big dinner.

9. _____ youngster was hit by _____ car while he was crossing the street.

10. What _____ bad weather we are having today.

11. He wants to hire _____ good housekeeper.

12. The lawyer gave his client _____ very good advice.

13. What _____ problem that was!

14. New York City has _____ large population.

6-3
ARTICLE vs. NO ARTICLE (2)

The is often used with a noncountable noun[2] *when the noun is followed by a modifier*.

The milk { which I bought a few days ago / left over from yesterday / in the refrigerator } should still be good.

but   Milk is good for children.
Fresh milk tastes good.

[2]See Exercise 1-5, pp. 6–8 for noncountable nouns.

Supply the article **the** if it is required. Give the reason why you did or did not use **the** with the noncountable nouns.

EXAMPLE: a. <u>The</u> genius of Edison is universally recognized. (*Genius* is followed by the modifier *of Edison*.)

              b. _ genius is 10% inspiration and 90% perspiration. (There is no modifier after *genius*.)

1. _____ bread has been called the staff of life.

2. _____ bread you baked is delicious.

3. _____ silver is used for money and jewelry.

4. _____ silver in this ring is of inferior quality.

5. He is studying _____ religion.

6. I would like to know more about _____ strange religion of these primitive people.

7. In order to survive, we must all have _____ food and _____ water.

8. _____ food in the restaurant near me is fairly good.

9. _____ water used in this beer comes from a special spring.

10. _____ psychology of birds and animals would be an interesting subject to study.

11. _____ psychology tells us a great deal about _____ human nature.

12. _____ smoke coming from the forest fire can be seen for miles around.

13. Where there's _____ smoke, there's _____ fire.

14. _____ baseball is the favorite sport of most Americans.

15. The American Constitution guarantees _____ life, _____ liberty, and _____ pursuit of happiness.

16. _____ transportation has always been a problem in that area because of the bad roads.

6-4
GENERIC USE OF ARTICLES

In a general statement, it is possible to use **the, a,** or no article with a concrete countable noun that represents a class.

The	**The lion is a wild animal.**	**The** emphasizes the *class itself*, without regard for concrete representatives of the class.
A	**A lion is a wild animal.**	**A** emphasizes an individual representative of a class. It has the sense of *any*.
No article	**Lions are wild animals.**	The plural form without an article emphasizes *all* the representatives of this class.

A. Use **the, a** or no article in the following general statements. (In some sentences, two choices are possible.)

EXAMPLE: a. Because of <u>the</u> automobile, man has extended his horizons, but he has poisoned the atmosphere.

          b. <u>An</u> automobile is a necessity today.

          c. <u>The</u> refrigerator has enabled people to keep food fresh for a much longer time.

1. _____ vegetables are good for the health.

2. The world is getting smaller because of _____ airplane.

3. _____ wheel and _____ plow were very important inventions.

4. _____ giraffe has a long neck.

5. _____ supermarket sells not only _____ groceries, but also _____ household items, _____ liquor, _____ plants, _____ magazines, and _____ candy.

6. _____ newspaper is one of the most widespread media of communication.

7. _____ tranquilizers, _____ sleeping pills, and _____ headache remedies are becoming part of our daily lives.

8. _____ computer is doing much of the work that used to be done by _____ human beings.

9. _____ engineer must have a good knowledge of mathematics and physics.

10. _____ modern conveniences have been of great help in _____ home.

11. It has been proven that _____ cigarettes are bad for the health.

12. _____ eagle is a bird of prey.

Since many general statements may be made with class words that are either singular or plural, it is often preferable to use the plural for persons so that further reference to the class word can be made with the pronoun **they,** which is neutral with respect to sex.

singular class word	A *student* should always try to do *his* (or *his or her*) best. (pronouns that are required by strict grammatical rules)
plural class word	*Students* should always try to do *their* best. (*their* refers to both males and females)

B. Change the singular class words to the plural. Use the required pronouns and make any other changes that are necessary. Do not use **the** with the plural class word.

EXAMPLE: A *good teacher* prepares *his* lesson thoroughly before *he* comes to class.

<u>*Good teachers* always prepare *their* lessons thoroughly before *they* come to class.</u>

1. A *child* requires a lot of love if *he* is to feel secure in later life.

_____

2. A *patriot* loves *his* country.

_____

3. An *engineer* must be able to apply *his* knowledge of mathematics and physics.

_____

4. An *elected official* should work for the good of the people *he* represents.

_____

5. A *salesperson* should always be courteous to *his* customers.

_____

6. A *doctor* has a great responsibility to *his* patients.

_____

7. These days a *store owner* must watch *his* merchandise carefully so that *he* is not robbed.

_____

8. An *employer* expects *his* employees to do a day's work for a day's pay.

_____

9. A *comedian* tries very hard to make *his* audience laugh.

_____

6-5
THE WITH NAMES FOR FAMILIAR OBJECTS

The occurs with names for familiar persons or objects in the home and the community. It is also used with names for natural objects in the world and in the universe. In these uses, **the** limits a noun to the one specimen *we are familiar with or that we have in mind*, although other specimens in the class may exist.

> He walked into **the** house and hung his coat in **the** closet.
> As she was strolling along **the** street she looked at **the** clothes in **the** store windows.
> They were sailing along **the** river watching **the** clouds in **the** sky.

In the following sentences, use **the** or **a**. Keep in mind that **a** refers to one unknown or unspecified person or thing, and that it is generally not used with a noncountable noun.

EXAMPLE: a. She ran into <u>the</u> house and shut <u>the</u> door.

b. They are planning to buy <u>a</u> house some day.

1. We have to feed _____ dog and _____ cat before we leave.

2. The boy has always wanted to have _____ dog and _____ cat.

3. This apartment has _____ bedroom, _____ living room, and _____ kitchen.

4. While he was in _____ park, he saw _____ man walking with _____ dog.

5. Everyone in _____ neighborhood was sorry to see them move.

6. They moved to _____ very quiet neighborhood.

7. Please put _____ butter, _____ bread, and _____ eggs in _____ refrigerator.

8. _____ refrigerator like theirs is very expensive.

9. He's going to _____ grocery store to buy _____ loaf of bread.

10. They live in _____ very expensive home.

11. _____ moon is _____ satellite of _____ earth.

12. He would rather swim in _____ ocean than in _____ sea.

13. She has an appointment this week with _____ doctor and _____ dentist.

14. _____ leaves are already falling off _____ trees and covering _____ ground.

15. The drugstore hired _____ new pharmacist.

6-6
THE WITH "RANKING" ADJECTIVES

1. **The** plus the superlatives of adjectives

> She is ***the best*** cook I know.
> They bought ***the most expensive*** furniture in the store.
> ***The richest*** are not always ***the happiest.***
> (Superlatives of adjectives used as nouns)

2. **The** plus ordinals

> ***the fifth*** row; ***the ninth*** day; ***the third*** chapter (but ***chapter three***)

3. **The** plus adjectives in a time or space sequence—the next, the following, the last

> A student in ***the last*** row was asleep.
> He arrived in town on Wednesday. On ***the next*** (or ***the following***) day he gave his lecture.

> Compare with: He will give his lecture ***next*** week.
> He gave his lecture ***last*** week.

4. **The** plus other adjectives that rank nouns—**chief, principal, main, only**

    The chief reason for his resignation was his bad health.

    He is *the only* person who can do this job.

A. Give the superlative of the word in parentheses.

EXAMPLE: a. She is (lazy) student in the class.
             She is the laziest student in the class.

             b. This is (delicious) cake I have ever tasted.
             This is the most delicious cake I have ever tasted.

1. He sometimes does (childish) things I have ever seen.

   _____

2. Go to Universal Printers; they will do (efficient) and (quick) job for you.

   _____

3. (successful) people are often those who are (ambitious).

   _____

4. (wealthy) people in the community contributed (much) money for the new wing of the hospital.

   _____

B. Give the ordinal of the figure in parentheses.

EXAMPLE: This is (5) year we have spent our vacation here.
             This is the fifth year we have spent our vacation here.

1. He has almost finished writing (9) chapter.

   _____

2. The meeting is scheduled for May (2). (*two possibilities*)

   _____

3. She bought (2) dress she tried on.

   _____

4. The office you're looking for is (3) door to the right.

   _____

5. She can never do anything right (1) time.

   _____

C. Use **the, a,** or no article with the word in parentheses.

EXAMPLE: This is (last) time I will ever shop in that store.
This is the last time I will ever shop in that store.

1. (last) week marked the beginning of the rainy season.

_____

2. On (last) week of the sale, prices were reduced still further.

_____

3. We are moving (next) month.

_____

4. The party lasted a long time. On (next) day everyone was tired.

_____

5. (only) excuse I can give for my rude behavior is that I was not feeling well.

_____

6. He made (only) one mistake.

_____

7. (only) restaurant that is open now is five miles from here.

_____

8. (chief) concern of this office is with legal matters.

_____

9. (principal) exports of that country are coffee and rubber.

_____

6-7
THE WITH GERUNDS OR ABSTRACT NOUNS

The is required before gerunds or abstract nouns that are followed by **of** phrases.

gerund	**The** instructing **of young children** is difficult.
	but Instructing young children is difficult.
abstract noun	**The** instruction **of young children** is difficult.

The gerund in a **the** + _____ + **of** construction is least common, and a true noun form, if it exists, is preferred in this construction.

Change the verbs in the parentheses to gerunds and/or abstract nouns. Be sure to use **the** if **of** follows the changed verb. If more than one choice is possible, determine which are preferable.

EXAMPLE: a, (imprison, people) without a trial is not part of the democratic process.

(The imprisoning of people, imprisoning people, the imprisonment of people) without a trial is not part of the democratic process. (the second and third choice are preferable.)

1.   (collect, garbage) is done by the Sanitation Department.

_____

2.   (invent, cotton gin) changed the economy of the South.

_____

3.   (standardize, the divorce laws) for all the states would be favored by many people in the United States.

_____

4.   (discover, new evidence) has brought about a postponement of his trial.

_____

5.   (shut down, the coal mines) caused great hardship in the town.

_____

6.   There was something about (describe, the robbery) by the victim that didn't seem quite right.

_____

7.   Her work as an editor is (revise, manuscripts).

_____

8.   (pronounce, that word) is very difficult.

_____

9.   (separate, the weaker students) from the better students will require a special diagnostic test.

_____

6-8
THE WITH PLACE NAMES (1)
GENERAL RULES

1.   **The** is used with names composed entirely or partially of common nouns. The last noun usually refers to a political union or association.

the Soviet Union, the United Kingdom,
the Dominican Republic, the British Commonwealth

2. **The** is used with names composed of common nouns plus proper nouns contained within **of** phrases.

the Republic of China, the Union of South Africa, the Gulf of Mexico,
the State of New York, the Lake of Geneva, the University of Pennsylvania

3. **The** is used with plural names.

the United States, the Philippine Islands,
the Rocky Mountains, the Great Lakes, the Balkans

4. **The** is used with names for special points on the globe.

the North Pole, the equator, the Southern Hemisphere

Supply **the** with place names wherever necessary. Be careful not to capitalize **the,** but note that words like **Republic, Gulf, Mountains** are capitalized.

1. _____ USSR stands for _____ Union of _____ Soviet Socialist Republics.

2. _____ Russia is the largest republic in _____ Soviet Union.

3. _____ United States is bordered on the east by _____ Canada and on the south by _____ Mexico and _____ Gulf of Mexico.

4. _____ Netherlands is another name for _____ Holland.

5. _____ Mount Vesuvius is still an active volcano.

6. _____ North Pole and _____ South Pole are on either extremity of the earth's axis.

7. _____ Pyrenees are situated between _____ France and _____ Spain.

8. _____ Ivory Coast, now an independent country, was once part of _____ French West Africa.

9. _____ Mount Everest has the highest elevation in the world.

10. _____ Himalayas have been referred to as "the roof of the world."

11. _____ Philippines, like other islands in _____ Malay Archipelago,[3] are the tops of drowned mountains protruding from the sea.

12. The earth is divided by _____ equator into _____ Northern Hemisphere and _____ Southern Hemisphere.

13. _____ Persia is now called _____ Iran.

14. _____ Dominican Republic is located in _____ Central America.

15. One slope of _____ Mt. Blanc is in _____ France, another in _____ Italy.

16. _____ Cuba and _____ Puerto Rico are in _____ West Indies.

17. _____ Great Lakes consist of five lakes in _____ Western Hemisphere.

[3]Use *the* with archipelago (a sea with many islands).

Place Names with *The*	Place Names without *The*

Most bodies of water:
  the Mississippi River
  the Pacific Ocean
  the Mediterranean Sea
  the English Channel
  the Panama Canal
  the Persian Gulf
    but the Gulf of Mexico
  the Bering Strait
(The *word* Ocean, Sea *or* River
may be omitted—the Mississippi)
Mountain ranges:
  the Rocky Mountains (The word *Mountains* may
  be omitted—the Rockies.)
No *the* with one mountain—Mount Everest, Bear
Mountain
Peninsulas:
  the Scandinavian Peninsula
Libraries, museums:
  the Louvre
  the Metropolitan Museum
  the Forty-Second Street Library
Points of the compass used as names for geographic
areas:
  the South, the Middle West, the Near East
    but Southern California
Hotels:
  the Statler Hotel
  the Carlyle Hotel
(The word **Hotel** may be omitted.)
	Continents:
	  Europe
	  Africa
	  North America
	Countries:
	  France, Peru, Japan
	    but the Sudan
	Cities, states:
	  Hong Kong, Buenos Aires, London, California,
	  Florida
	    but the Hague, the Vatican
	Lakes, bays, capes, waterfalls:
	  Lake Michigan
	  Cape Cod
	  Hudson Bay
	    but the Bay of Biscay
	Islands:
	  Coney Island, Wake Island
	    but the Philippine Islands (the word **Islands** may
	    be omitted—the Philippines)
	Universities, colleges:
	  Columbia University
	    but the University of California
	Streets, avenues, boulevards:
	  Pennsylvania Avenue
	  Forty-second Street
	Parks:
	  Hyde Park, Central Park

Supply **the** wherever needed.

1. _____ Amazon is the largest river system in the world, but _____ Nile is the longest river.

2. _____ North America is bounded on the east by _____ Atlantic Ocean and on the west by _____ Pacific Ocean.

3. A few seas have the names of colors: _____ Black Sea, _____ Red Sea, _____ Yellow Sea.

4. _____ Suez Canal is in _____ Middle East.

5. On a plateau bordering ———— Peru and ———— Bolivia ———— is ———— Lake Titicaca, the highest navigable lake in the world.

6. ———— Allegheny Mountains are in the eastern part of ———— North America.

7. ———— St. Petersburg is now called ———— Leningrad.

8. ———— Far East, or ———— Orient, refers to the area of ———— Asia where ———— China and ———— Japan are located.

9. He used to live in ———— South, but then he moved to ———— California.

10. ———— Balkan Peninsula is surrounded by ———— Black Sea and ———— Adriatic, Ionian, and Aegean Seas of ———— Mediterranean.

11. ———— Russia and ———— Alaska almost meet at ———— Bering Strait.

12. ———— Brazil covers nearly half the continent of ———— South America.

13. ———— Norway and ———— Sweden occupy ———— Scandinavian Peninsula; ———— Portugal and ———— Spain comprise ———— Iberian Peninsula.

14. ———— Strait of Gibraltar separates ———— Europe from ———— Africa.

15. Tea is grown in many parts of ———— southern Asia, especially in ———— India and ———— Ceylon.

16. ———— British Museum houses an immense library.

17. ———— Louvre and ———— Metropolitan Museum are both world-famous.

18. ———— New York Stock Exchange is located on ———— Wall Street.

19. ———— Columbia University, ———— Princeton University, and ———— Yale University are all regarded as excellent American universities.

20. There are many beautiful shops on ———— Fifth Avenue in ———— New York.

21. ———— Central Park is right in the heart of ———— New York City.

22. ———— Royal Hawaiian Hotel is one of the oldest in ———— Honolulu.

23. ———— Downing Street is a famous street in ———— London.

24. ———— Hudson Valley[4] is very fertile.

6-10
THE WITH WORDS OF TIME AND PLACE

Time

1. Points in a progression—**the beginning, the middle, the end**
2. Points in a time continuum—**the past, the present, the future** (but **at present**)

[4]The name of a valley is used with **the.**

3. Parts of the day—**in the morning, in the afternoon, in the evening** (*but* **at noon, at midnight**)

4. Seasons—**in the winter** (*or* **summer, autumn, spring**). **The** is sometimes omitted here, especially in a general statement—**In (the) winter we go skiing in the Alps.**

5. Time expressions meaning **this**—**at the** (= **this**) **moment, for the time being, during the year, all the while**

Place

the top, the bottom, the middle

the back, the front, the side, the center

the inside (*or* interior), the outside (*or* exterior)

No article is used with nouns denoting certain places in the environment.

He is going to {
church.
school *or* elementary school, high school, college, but **the** university.
prison, *or* jail.

He is going {
home.
downtown.

Supply the where needed.

1. At _____ beginning, he couldn't get used to the food.

2. At _____ first, she didn't like her English teacher, but toward _____ middle of the semester she began to appreciate him.

3. Don't worry so much about _____ future; it _____ present that is most important.

4. He takes his lunch at _____ noon.

5. In _____ middle of the road sat a puppy who would not budge at the sound of the horn.

6. The point the author was trying to make was stated at _____ beginning of the book.

7. _____ inside of the house was gaily decorated for the party. However there were no decorations _____ outside.

8. Many of the chief characters in the play die at _____ end.

9. She is taking several history courses at _____ present.

10. He is on the telephone at _____ present moment.

11. They went _____ downtown to do some shopping.

12. These flowers bloom in _____ spring.

13. Her youngest son is now going to _____ high school. He hopes to go to _____ university next year.

14. He can't fall asleep at _____ night if there is any noise.

15. During _____ night there was a great deal of noise outside our window.

6-11
THE WITH WORDS
REFERRING TO EVENTS, GOVERNMENT

1. Names of historical periods or events—**the Ming Dynasty, the Middle Ages, the Renaissance, the French Revolution, the Civil War, the First World War** (*but* **World War II**).
2. Names of bills, acts, and other legislative deliberations—**the Magna Carta, the Taft-Hartley Bill, the Missouri Compromise.**
3. Official titles—**the Secretary of State, the Foreign** (*or* **Prime**) **Minister, the King, the Premier,** (but no *the* if the name accompanies the title—**President Washington**).
4. Law enforcement bodies, civil and military—**the Army, the Navy, the Air Corps, the state militia, the police, the highway patrol.**
5. Names of branches of the government—**the executive** (*or* **the legislative, the judicial**) **branch.**
6. Names of institutions, foundations, organizations—**the United Nations, the Ford Foundation, the Girl Scouts.**
7. Names of political parties—**the Labor party, the Conservative party, the Democratic party, the Communist party.** The name of the party is often used in the plural without the word **party—the Democrats, the Republicans, the Conservatives.**

Articles are generally not used with names of holidays—**Thanksgiving, Christmas, Easter,** *but*—**the Fourth of July.**

Supply **the** where needed.

1. Da Vinci painted during _____ Italian Renaissance.

2. _____ World War Two ended in 1945.

3. _____ Industrial Revolution brought about great changes in western civilization.

4. _____ American Constitution guarantees freedom of speech.

5. _____ President of the United States and _____ Prime Minister of England are both heads of state.

6. _____ Parliament is not in session today.

7. _____ Navy reported the loss of two ships.

8. _____ police are holding two men on suspicion of murder.

9. _____ Thanksgiving is celebrated at the end of November.

10. _____ legislative branch of the government makes the laws; _____ executive branch carries them out.

11. He belongs to _____ Democratic party.

12. _____ President Nixon made many speeches in _____ Congress.

13. _____ Supreme Court is going to announce their decision on this case soon.

14. _____ Monroe Doctrine stated that European countries were not to interfere in the affairs of Latin America.

15. _____ Election Day in the United States occurs on the Tuesday after the first Monday in November.

6-12

THE IN *OF* PHRASES AFTER WORDS EXPRESSING QUANTITY

A determiner is required in an **of** phrase after a word of indefinite quantity or after a numeral. This determiner is usually **the.**

Most
All
Many } of **the** students (in this class) passed the examination.
One-third
Five
The majority

Often, **of the** makes the situation specific. If there is no desire to be specific, **of the** may be omitted.

Most
Many } students (in this class) passed the examination.
Five

In general statements without modifiers after the nouns, **of** is not used.

Most students want to get good grades.

Rewrite the words in parentheses by adding *of the* or nothing. In sentences where two choices are possible, give both choices.

EXAMPLE: a. (Many) <u>many, many of the</u> people in the room were protesting against the new regulations.

         b. (Many) <u>many</u> people were in the room.   Insert Underscore, msp.

1. (Most) _____ clerical mistakes are the result of carelessness.

2. (Most) _____ clerical mistakes in our office could be avoided if the clerks paid more attention to their work.

3. (Some) _____ students are lazy.

4. (Some) _____ students I know are lazy.

5. (Many) _____ arguments have been presented for equality before the law.

6. (Many) _____ arguments presented by his lawyer were very powerful.

7. (Both)[5] _____ men who were charged with disorderly conduct were fined by the judge.

[5]With **both, all, half,** the word **of** may be omitted before **the**—all **(of) the** students in the class).

8.   (Very few) _____ men would be as patient with a nagging wife as he is.

9.   (Four) _____ passengers in the car were hurt in the accident.

10.   (All) _____ men are created equal.

11.   (All) _____ men who have been accused will be given a fair trial.

12.   (Most) _____ juvenile delinquency occurs because young people are not supervised by their parents.

13.   In (some) _____ developing countries, (many) _____ people from the villages come to the cities to look for work.

14.   (Most) _____ young children would rather play than study.

6-13
THE IN CONSTRUCTIONS LIKE *THE MORE, THE MERRIER*

This older type of construction is still in common use today. **The** may appear adverbially with single words or with whole clauses.

> **The** more, ***the*** merrier.
> **The** harder he works, ***the*** less he succeeds.
> **The** prettier the girl (is), ***the*** more foolishly he behaves.

Note that the **comparative** form appears after each **the** in this construction.

Change each sentence into a **the . . . the** construction.

EXAMPLE: a.   If the challenge is great, he likes it more.
              <u>The greater the challenge (is), the more he likes it.</u>

              b.   As they argued, they became angrier.
              <u>The more they argued, the angrier they became.</u>

1.   If he spends less money now, he'll have more later.

_____

2.   If he comes sooner, this will be better. (Use only **the better** in the second part.)

_____

3.   If we get to the theater later, we'll get worse seats.

_____

4.   If a restaurant is large, its service is more impersonal.

_____

5. If we do more work now, we'll have less to do later.

_____

6. If you take less baggage, you'll be better off.

_____

7. As he worked longer, his job became easier.

_____

8. As he sees her more, he likes her more.

_____

9. As he grew older, he became more eccentric.

_____

10. As she did more for him, he complained more.

_____

11. As she cooks more, she becomes better.

_____

12. As he learns more about life, he becomes more cynical.

_____

13. As prices rose higher, the workers asked for more money.

_____

14. As he earned more money, he spent more.

_____

6-14
OTHER USES OF *THE*

The is used:

1. to narrow down a class to *only one*.
   This is **the** way to do it. (This is the only way.)
   but This is **a** good way to do it. (This is one of several ways.)
2. to refer back to something previously mentioned.
   A strange dog came on the porch.
   The dog seemed very friendly.
3. with class words for social or other institutions
   the home, **the** family, **the** church, **the** government, **the** young generation
   but society
4. with names of newspapers—The *New York Times*, but usually not with magazines—*Time Magazine*
5. after **play**, for an instrument—play **the** piano, play **the** violin

6. with certain illnesses
   She has **the** flu (or **the** mumps, **the** measles)
   but She has a cold (or a sore throat, a headache, a virus)
   She has heart trouble, (or polio, pneumonia)

Use the, a or nothing.

EXAMPLE: a. <u>The</u> measles is a contagious disease.

b. He was <u>the</u> only person who witnessed the crime.

c. In many countries, <u>the</u> home and <u>the</u> family are no longer the sacred institutions they once were.

1. Washington, D.C. is _____ capital of the United States.

2. Last year they bought _____ new house. _____ house is located near a park.

3. In some countries, _____ church was once just as powerful as _____ state.

4. One of the best newspapers in Great Britain is _____ *London Times*.

5. He has had _____ heart trouble ever since he was a child.

6. The bride said she was looking forward to having _____ home and _____ family.

7. He is writing _____ new book. _____ book is about the Civil War in the United States.

8. In the sixties, _____ young generation rebelled against all the demands of _____ society.

9. _____ *Wall Street Journal* gives important financial news.

10. Their child has _____ flu. She has _____ sore throat and _____ bad headache.

11. They have one son who plays _____ violin and another who plays _____ flute.

12. Many women like to read _____ *Vogue* for the latest news about fashion.

13. She has been playing _____ piano since she was a child.

6-15
INDEFINITE *A* vs. INDEFINITE *SOME*

Corresponding to indefinite **a** used with singular countable nouns is indefinite **some** used with plural nouns or with noncountable nouns.

> I need _____<u>a</u>_____ chair. (singular countable noun)
> I need _____<u>some</u>_____ chairs. (plural countable noun)
> I need _____<u>some</u>_____ furniture. (noncountable noun)

In such indefinite use, it is possible to omit **some** but not **a.**

Use a or some.

EXAMPLE: a. She wants <u>some</u> stationery. (noncountable noun)

          b. She wants <u>some</u> pencils. (plural noun)

          c. She wants <u>a</u> pencil. (singular countable noun)

1. They are building _____ new house.

2. Isn't tomorrow _____ holiday?

3. Please give me _____ information about this university.

4. I would like _____ toast and _____ cup of coffee.

5. They are planning to buy _____ expensive camera.

6. _____ children were playing in the school yard when _____ explosion was heard.

7. I need _____ hammer and _____ nails.

8. She has just bought _____ new clothes.

9. Can you lend me _____ pair of scissors?

10. A good lawyer can give you _____ advice about that matter.

6-16
INDEFINITE A vs. CLASSIFYING A

Indefinite **a** and classifying **a** may be distinguished from each other by their different plurals.

	Singular	Plural
Indefinite **a**	*He ate **an** apple.*	*He ate **some** apples.*
Classifying **a**	*He is **a** good student.* ***A** lion is very strong.*	*They are good **students.*** ***Lions** are very strong.*

Note that **some** is used with the plural of indefinite **a**, but not with the plural of classifying **a**.

Change the following sentences by using the plural of the italicized words. Make whatever other changes are necessary.

EXAMPLE: a. A *student* was writing on the blackboard.
<u>Some students were writing on the blackboard.</u>

          b. A *horse* is an *animal*.
<u>Horses are animals.</u>

1. He was excited about a beautiful *bird* he had just seen.

2. There is a *river* in this region.

_____

3. A *river* is a *body of water*.

_____

4. This recipe requires an *egg*.

_____

5. An *egg* should be eaten fresh.

_____

6. We received an important *letter* yesterday.

_____

7. An *applicant* for the job was waiting to be interviewed.

_____

8. A *demagogue* tries to gain political power by playing on people's emotions.

_____

9. *She* is a hard-working *nurse*.

_____

10. A *pigeon* flew into the room.

_____

11. A *horse* has a *mane* and a *tail*.

_____

12. A *monarchy* is ruled by a *king* or a *queen*.

_____

13. A *carrot* is a yellow vegetable.

_____

6-17
CLASSIFYING A

A. Use a sentence placing each word in the smaller class into one of the words in the larger class. Use the dictionary if necessary.

Smaller Class	*Larger Class*
1. monkey	bird
2. lettuce	flower
3. bee	continent
4. bronze	gas
5. lily	kind of wine

6.	nitrogen	animal
7.	Africa	car
8.	Cadillac	industry
9.	newspaper	insect
10.	parrot	article of clothing
11.	champagne	metal
12.	belt	vegetable
13.	coal mining	medium of communication

EXAMPLE: a. <u>A monkey is an animal.</u>

b. <u>Lettuce is a vegetable.</u>

B. Note which words in the smaller class can also be used with **the** (usually names of species of insects, birds, plants, animals).

C. Change all the sentences from A into the plural, if possible.

EXAMPLE: a. <u>Monkeys are animals.</u>

b. <u>no change possible with noncountable **lettuce.**</u>

6-18
WHAT (A), *SUCH* (A)

What a and **such a** occur only with singular countable nouns, not with plural or noncountable nouns.

Change into sentences with **what** and **such.**

EXAMPLE: a. Mary, is, pretty girl. (singular countable noun)
<u>What a pretty girl Mary is.</u>

<u>Mary is such a pretty girl.</u>

b. They, are, pretty girls. (plural countable noun)
<u>What pretty girls they are.</u>

<u>They are such pretty girls.</u>

c. Mary, has, pretty hair. (noncountable noun)
<u>What pretty hair Mary has.</u>

<u>Mary has such pretty hair.</u>

1. She, is, good cook.

2. She, has, expensive furniture.

_____

_____

3. We, are having, fine weather.

_____

_____

4. This, is, hot climate.

_____

_____

5. It, is, cold day.

_____

_____

6. They, are gathering, useless information.

_____

_____

7. This car, has, powerful motor.

_____

_____

8. She, has, long eyelashes.

_____

_____

9. They, are, helpless people.

_____

_____

10. We, saw, beautiful rainbow.

_____

_____

11. This, is, fancy restaurant.

_____

_____

12. She, has, good taste.

_____

_____

13. He, made, rude remark.

_____

_____

14. The children, are wearing, dirty clothes.

_____

_____

15. This, is, tasteless food.

_____

_____

6-19
A WITH NOUNS THAT ARE
BOTH COUNTABLE AND NONCOUNTABLE

Some nouns that are derived from verbs may have both a countable and a noncountable use. The noncountable word refers to the act itself—**operation, imitation, government**—and the countable word refers to the concrete product or the result of the act—**an operation, an imitation, a government.**

The child learns through imitation.

but $\begin{cases} \text{Art is an imitation of life.} \\ \text{This picture is a good imitation.} \end{cases}$

Supply the article **a** wherever it indicates the concrete product or the result of an act.

EXAMPLE: a. The electric light was <u>an</u> important invention.

b. _ necessity is the mother of _ invention.

1. That painting is _____ possession he dearly prizes.

2. For the hedonist, _____ pleasure is considered the greatest good.

3. Meeting you has been _____ great pleasure.

4. Their landlord always gives them _____ receipt for the rent.

5. _____ growth and _____ maturation are important processes of _____ life.

6. Everyone would like to be free from _____ pain.

7. She told the doctor she had _____ pain in her back.

8. _____ variety is the spice of _____ life.

9. The salesman showed her _____ variety of shoes.

10. The Stoics felt we should calmly accept our fate without expressing _____ grief or

_____ joy.

11. She checked with the doctor about _____ tiny growth on her chin.

12. _____ revolution is going on right now in that country.

13. The doctor told him he might need _____ operation on his leg.

14. Everyone who admires _____ democracy would like to live in _____ democracy.

6-20
A WITH NONCOUNTABLE NOUNS

In some sentences, noncountable abstract nouns with *adjective modifiers* may be used with **a** rather than with **the**. In many such sentences **a** is the equivalent of **a kind of** and has general reference, whereas **the** has specific reference.

> He exhibited **a** courage **that surprised me.**
> *vs.* **The** courage **that he exhibited** surprised me.
>
> We encountered **an unexpected friendliness** wherever we went.
> *vs.* **The** unexpected friendliness **that we encountered** wherever we went was very gratifying.

Use **a** or **the** with the abstract nouns. Remember that **a** means **a kind of** and has general reference and that **the** has specific reference.

EXAMPLE: a. He displayed _a_ wisdom far beyond his years.

b. _The_ wisdom he displayed was far beyond his years.

1. He has _____ simplicity which is seldom met with these days.

2. They live in _____ atmosphere of never-ceasing anxiety.

3. _____ atmosphere he creates in his novels is of never-ceasing anxiety.

4. He has _____ aversion to any kind of work.

5. _____ aversion he felt for any kind of work was unbelievable.

6. She enjoys _____ popularity which is well deserved.

7. He never told anyone about _____ loneliness he had experienced in the big city.

8. In the big city, he experienced _____ loneliness which he had never known before.

9. _____ knowledge of history gives us _____ sense of perspective.

10. He felt _____ awareness of _____ hopelessness of his situation.

11. _____ better understanding of the problem will help us to solve it.

12. Everyone was impressed by _____ sincerity with which he spoke.

13. She has never forgotten _____ advice she received from her father.

14. He has had _____ excellent education in one of the best universities.

6-21
ARTICLES IN IDIOMS WITH VERBS

Some verbs form idioms with their objects. Sometimes **a** is used with the object, sometimes **the**, and sometimes no article at all.

1. *A* with the object—**do a favor, tell a lie, make a living, make a remark, take a trip, take a picture, become a reality, play a joke on, call a halt, take a look at, make a mistake**
2. *The* with the object—**make the beds, clear the table, wash the dishes, tell the truth**
3. *No article* with the object—**make friends with, take care of, take revenge on, shake hands, take pride in, take part in, take notice of, have faith in, take pity on, take advantage of, make fun of.**

Use **a, the,** *or* leave blank.

1. He made _____ mistake in his addition.

2. Space travel has now become _____ reality.

3. He makes _____ friends with people very easily.

4. He often makes _____ fun of people or takes _____ advantage of them.

5. We should always try to tell _____ truth, but sometimes it is better to tell _____ little white lie.

6. He makes _____ living by writing books.

7. She has taken _____ part in many amateur theatrical productions.

8. When he took _____ trip to India, he took _____ picture of the Taj Mahal.

9. He takes _____ pride in his country and has _____ faith in it.

10. I must clear _____ table and wash _____ dishes before we can go out.

11. Let's call _____ halt to this bitter argument and shake _____ hands.

12. Would you do me _____ favor and make _____ beds for me?

13. The close observation of other planets is now becoming _____ reality.

14. The company takes _____ care of all the traveling expenses of its salesmen.

REVIEW OF ARTICLES

A. Supply **a** or **an** where needed.

1. He does not have _____ single regret about what he did.

2. He made _____ bad mistake in his report.

3. New York City has _____ large population.

4. She wants to become _____ nurse.

5. _____ youngster was hit by _____ car while he was crossing the street.

6. _____ engineer must have _____ good knowledge of mathematics and physics.

7. Please give me _____ information about this university.

8. Isn't tomorrow _____ holiday?

9. The boy has always wanted to have _____ dog.

10. She has such _____ expensive furniture.

11. What _____ fine weather we are having.

12. The electric light was _____ important invention.

13. Everyone would like to be free from _____ pain.

14. _____ demagogue tries to gain political power by playing on people's emotions.

15. They are planning to buy _____ expensive camera.

16. He makes _____ living by writing books.

B. Supply **the** where needed.

1. He is studying _____ religion.

2. In order to survive, we must all have _____ food and _____ water.

3. _____ psychology tells us a great deal about _____ human nature.

4. _____ smoke coming from _____ forest fire can be seen for miles around.

5. _____ baseball is _____ favorite sport of _____ most Americans.

6. _____ vegetables are good for _____ health.

7. The world is getting smaller because of _____ airplane.

8. It has been proven that _____ cigarettes are bad for _____ health.

9. _____ eagle is a bird of prey.

10. She is _____ laziest student in _____ class.

11. This is _____ most delicious cake I have ever tasted.

12. They can never do anything right _____ first time.

13. _____ American Constitution guarantees freedom of speech.

14. John is _____ only student who didn't pass _____ test.

15. He was arrested for _____ resisting a police officer in _____ course of his duty.

16. There was something about _____ description of _____ robbery by _____ victim that didn't seem right.

17. _____ conquest of England by _____ Normans took place in 1066.

18. _____ standardizing the divorce laws for all the states would be favored by many people.

19. _____ Russia is _____ largest republic in _____ Soviet Union.

20. _____ United States is bordered on _____ east by _____ Canada and on _____ south by _____ Mexico and _____ Gulf of Mexico.

21. _____ North Pole and _____ South Pole are on either extremity of _____ earth's axis.

22. _____ Suez Canal is in _____ Middle East.

23. _____ Allegheny Mountains are in _____ eastern part of _____ North America.

24. He used to live in _____ South, but then he moved to _____ California.

25. _____ Strait of Gilbralter separates _____ Europe from _____ Africa.

26. _____ British Museum houses an immense library.

27. _____ New York Stock Exchange is located on _____ Wall Street.

28. _____ Central Park is right in the heart of _____ New York City.

29. _____ World War Two ended in 1945.

30. _____ most young children would rather play than study.

31. _____ invention of _____ cotton gin changed _____ economy of _____ South.

C. Change each sentence into a **the . . . the** construction.

1. If we get to the theater later, we'll get worse seats.

   _____

2. If we do more work now, we'll have less to do later.

   _____

3. As he worked longer, his job became easier.

   _____

4. As he learns more about life, he becomes more cynical.

   _____

5. As prices rose higher, the workers asked for more money.

   _____

7

Adverbs

STRUCTURAL DESCRIPTION OF ADVERBS

Types of Adverbs and Function	Position of Adverbs	Form of Adverbs

1. *Manner*—modifies the verb
quickly
awkwardly
2. *Place and direction*—*modifies* the verb
here, away, outside, left, straight, west
3. *Time*—modifies the verb
  a. definite
    today
    yesterday
    tomorrow
  b. indefinite
    recently
    later
    always
4. *Intensifying*
  a. degree—modifies an adjective or adverb
    very (strong)
    quite (frequently)
  b. emphasizing—modifies all parts of speech
    even (she)
    only (once)
5. *Conjunctive adverb*—modifies the sentence
therefore
nevertheless
6. *Sentence adverb*—modifies the sentence
fortunately
actually
	1. *Initial position*
	Sometimes she comes late.
	(position of greatest emphasis)
	2. *Mid-position* (with verb)
	She sometimes comes late.
	3. *Final position*
	She comes late sometimes.
		1. *Grammatical* (for comparison)
		  a. *more . . . than*
		    more quickly than
		    the most . . .
		    the most quickly
		  b. *. . . -er than* (for short adverbs often having the same form as adjectives)
		    faster than
		    the . . . -est
		    the fastest
		2. *Derivational*
		Mostly **-ly** added to adjectives
		quickly
		extremely
		Two or more words may combine to form an adverbial word group—**so far, the day before yesterday, as a matter of fact.**
		
		Markers of Adverbs
		Degree intensifiers
		  very, quite, etc.

Although it is possible for an adverb or an adverbial word group to occupy initial position, mid-position with the verb, or final position, all three positions are not always possible for each type of adverb. The more common positions for the different types of adverbs are as follows.

Adverbs of manner	*final position* *but* also: mid-position initial position	She dances very **gracefully.** She **quickly** left the room. **Quickly,** he took out his gun and fired.
Adverbs of place and direction	*final position* *but* also: initial position	It's cold **outside.** **Outside,** it was bitterly cold.
Adverbs of time definite	*final position* *but* also: initial position	The ship will arrive **tomorrow.** **Tomorrow,** we will leave for Chicago.
indefinite	*mid-position* *but* also: initial position final position	They were **recently** married. **Recently,** the news about the nation's economy has not been good. We have been having many strikes **recently.**
Conjunctive adverbs	*Initial position* *or* *mid-position* *but* also: final position	The motor you sent is defective; **therefore,** we are returning it to you. . . . ; we are **therefore** returning it to you. . . . ; we are returning it to you **therefore.**
Sentence adverbs	*initial position* *but* also: mid-position final position	Two cars collided at that intersection; **fortunately,** no one was hurt. . . . ; no one, **fortunately,** was hurt. . . . ; no one was hurt, **fortunately.**

Final position is used with conjunctive adverbs and sentence adverbs only if what precedes them is short.

Intensifiers appear directly before the words they modify—**It is very (or quite, rather, extremely) cold outside.**

Commas used with adverbials are often optional; such commas usually represent a pause in speech.

Place the adverbials in parentheses in the most usual position. Note other possible positions for these adverbials. Keep in mind that initial position is the position of greatest emphasis.

1.   (quietly) The nurse moved from one patient to another.

_____

2.   (mysteriously) One of his valuable paintings disappeared.

_____

3.   (outside) There are some people waiting.

_____

4.   (ten years ago) There were only private homes in this neighborhood.

_____

5.   (in a few years) We may be able to send a man to Mars.

_____

6.   (today) (on the doorstep) The milkman didn't put any milk.

_____

7.   (now) Let's not do the dishes. (later) We can do them.

_____

8.   (for a long time) I haven't seen him.

_____

9.   (always) He has been working for the government.

_____

10. (quite) The boy is insolent to his mother.

_____

11. (nearly) The work is finished.

_____

12. (obviously) He doesn't want to lose any money in this business deal.

_____

13. (definitely) I saw someone hiding behind those bushes.

_____

14. He didn't feel he had a chance to be accepted by one of the large universities; (therefore) he decided to apply to the small college near his home.

_____

ADVERBS IN MID-POSITION
(WITH THE VERB)

The position of an adverb with the verb varies according to the number of auxiliaries that accompany the verb.

		Usual Position of Adverb	Sentences
1.	*Verbs with no auxiliaries* (Simple present and simple past tenses) a. *the verb* **be** b. *all other verbs*	*after the verb* *before the verb*	She is **sometimes** late. She **sometimes** comes late.
2.	*Verbs with one to three auxiliaries*	*after the first auxiliary*	She has **sometimes** come late. She has **sometimes** been coming late.

A less usual position for an adverb in mid-position is before the independent verb **be** or the first auxiliary.

> She sometimes is late.
>
> She sometimes has come late.
>
> She sometimes has been coming late.

An adverb of manner (or completion) must be put directly before the verb, regardless of the number of auxiliaries.

> The experiment has been **carefully** planned.
>
> The prices of the merchandise will be **sharply** reduced.

An important rule to remember about an adverb in mid-position is that it is generally not placed between the verb and its object.[1]

Place the adverb in parentheses in *the most usual position* with the verb. Be careful not to place an adverb between a verb and its object. Note where a second position with the verb is possible.

1. (frequently) They were absent from school.

_____

2. (usually) He is calm and even-tempered.

_____

[1]However, an adverb of manner may appear before a long object—**Please read carefully all the sections in the book that deal with adverbs.**

3. (almost never) She loses her temper.

_____

4. (seldom) She leaves the children unattended.

_____

5. (usually) This disease is fatal; (seldom) patients recover from it.

_____

6. (first) The robber made sure that no one was looking before (stealthily) he crept through the window.

_____

7. (systematically) The retreating army blew up all the bridges behind them.

_____

8. (always) They have expressed the same opinion about everything.

_____

9. (completely) He has misunderstood what I have been saying.

_____

10. (falsely) The servant has been accused of stealing the jewelry.

_____

11. (probably) He will take the dog to the veterinarian today.

_____

12. (utterly) Their house was ruined by the flood.

_____

13. (evidently) She has been interfering in all her son's affairs.

_____

14. (recently) He has been invited to give a talk on data processing.

_____

15. (thoroughly) The case is being investigated.

_____

7-3
ADVERBIALS IN FINAL POSITION

An adverb or adverbial word group used in final position appears after the verb and any complement(s) it may have. If more than one adverbial occurs in final position, the usual order is **place, manner, time.**

1 Subject	2 Verb + Complement	3 Place	4 Manner also in This Position: Instrument, Agent, Accompaniment, Degree	5 Frequency	6 Other Kinds of Time
I	appreciate him		more and more (*degree*)	each time I see him.	
She	cut the bread		slowly (*manner*) with a dull knife. (*instrument*)		
He	was walking	along the street	quietly (*manner*) with his dog (*accompaniment*)		last night.
This toy	may be made	at home	by young people (*agent*) very easily (*manner*) with a few simple tools. (*instrument*)		
They	put the box	in a dry place			during the storm.
Mr. Lee	visited his wife	in the hospital		every day	for a month last year.

Actually, there is some degree of flexibility in the sequence of adverbials in final position. A general rule seems to be that a shorter adverbial precedes a longer one. However, a one-word adverbial of place like **here, there, away,** usually remains closest to the verb, and an adverbial of definite time like **today, yesterday** generally comes last.

Adverbials expressing *purpose*, especially infinitives, often follow other adverbials in final position—**We'll call a meeting next week to discuss his proposal.**

Arrange each of the following so that all adverbials are in final position. In some sentences there may be more than one acceptable arrangement of adverbials. Be careful not to separate a verb and its object. Do not use commas with these adverbials in final position.

EXAMPLE: at all times, a guard, there, is, in the building.
<u>There is a guard in the building at all times.</u>

1. on the line, the clothes, hangs, she, early in the morning.

———————————————————————————

2. at the same cafeteria, eat, at exactly the same time, they, every day.

———————————————————————————

3. he, to the post office, to mail the letters, at 5:00 P.M., his office boy, sent.

———————————————————————————

4. very enthusiastically, the last time I saw him, spoke, he, about the new play.

_____

5. hastily, while he was waiting for her, something, wrote, he, on a piece of paper.

_____

6. after the trial, the lawyer, everyone, highly, commended.

_____

7. hesitantly, walked, the defendant, into the courtroom.

_____

8. impatiently, waited, for the play to begin, the audience.

_____

9. the two sides, exchanged, across the border, all through the night, gunfire.

_____

10. for three hours, must simmer, the stew, slowly.

_____

11. into their new house, the day before yesterday, moved, they.

_____

12. to Hong Kong, he, is going, to buy some jade, with his wife.

_____

13. very well, speaks, when he's not tired, English, he.

_____

7-4
REVERSAL OF WORD ORDER
AFTER CERTAIN ADVERBIALS

The subject and verb are often reversed after (1) initial negatives (or near negatives), (2) initial **only, so** or **such,** (3) initial expressions of place. Such a reversal, which permits more emphasis to be placed on the adverbial, often represents formal usage.

A. Reversal After Initial Negatives (or Near Negatives)

Never	have	I	seen	such a sight.
Seldom	did	they	have	enough to eat.
No sooner	had	he	left	the office than he received an important telephone call.

Note that the reversal is between the subject and the auxiliary, as in questions. If there is no auxiliary, the **do** auxiliary is used.

The negative conjunctions **not only, nor, neither** also require such reversals.

> Not only is his new car less expensive then the old one, but it also uses less gasoline.
>
> She doesn't know where her former husband is living, nor does she care to know.

Move the italicized negative or near-negative elements to the beginning of the sentence. Be sure to reverse the order of subject and verb.

EXAMPLE: a. He had *never* been allowed to do as he pleased.
               <u>Never had he been allowed to do as he pleased.</u>

            b. There has been *no* complete justice *at any time in history*. (Use *at no time in history*.)
               <u>At no time in history has there been complete justice.</u>

1. You will *never again* have another opportunity like this.

_____

2. He did *not* complain *once* about his financial difficulties.

_____

3. He had *scarcely* entered the room when he was greeted by the host and hostess.

_____

_____

4. He *never* failed to bring his wife a gift for her birthday.

_____

_____

5. He has *not, on any occasion*, disregarded the rights of the workers. (Use *on no occasion*.)

_____

_____

6. There will *seldom* be any need for such an extreme measure.

_____

_____

7. I would *never in the world* care to go through that terrible experience again.

_____

_____

8. The factory *not only* had a burglar alarm system, but it had a watchman patrolling the grounds day and night.

_____

_____

9. This door is *not* to be unlocked *at any time*. (Use *at no time*.)

_____

10. They have never traveled to a foreign country. They do *not* expect to do so in the future. (Begin the second sentence with *nor*.)

_____

_____

11. The couple had *no sooner* returned home than a neighbor knocked on their door.

_____

_____

12. There were *not only* prizes for everyone, but there was a grand prize for the lucky winner.[2]

_____

B. Reversal After Initial *ONLY, SO* or *SUCH*

Only once	did	she	complain about the amount of work she had to do.
So extensive	was	the damage	that the house had to be completely rebuilt.
Such a powerful man	was	he	that no one dared to oppose him.

Move the italicized words to the beginning of the sentence. Make the necessary reversal of subject and verb.

EXAMPLE: a. We get a chance to go camping *only once in a while*.

        Only once in a while do we get a chance to go camping.

      b. She entered the room *so silently* that no one noticed her.

        So silently did she enter the room that no one noticed her.

      c. He realized how much she meant to him *only when he had lost her*.

        Only when he had lost her did he realize how much she meant to him.

1. This exit is to be used *only in the event of fire*.

_____

2. I will consent to see him *only if he apologizes*.

_____

[2]As with questions, a single form of the independent verb *be* does not require the *do* auxiliary—**Not only is he rich, but he is very rich.**

3. He realized what a tremendous task he had accomplished *only after the mural was completed*.

_____

_____

4. An exception can be made *only in rare cases*.

_____

5. His answers were *so circumspect* that no useful information could be learned from them.

_____

_____

6. They were *such rare birds* that they had not even been recorded in any book.

_____

_____

7. The fire spread *so rapidly* that it took many days to get it under control.

_____

_____

C. Reversal After Initial Expressions of Place

There	stood	the tallest man he had ever seen.
Before them	lay	a vast expanse of desert.
Inside the room	were	a few dilapidated pieces of furniture.
Among those present	were	the governor and his wife.

Such reversals often occur with the verbs **be, stand, lie, sit,** but may also occur with other verbs. The auxiliary **do** is not used in reversals after place; also the parts of a passive verb are not separated—**In the box** *was found* **a large sum of money.**

Not all initial adverbs of place require a reversal of subject and verb—**In his hand he held a small round object.**

Move the italicized adverbials of place to the beginning of the sentence. Make the necessary reversal of subject and verb. (In a few sentences a reversal is not required but is preferable to avoid ending a sentence with a verb.)

EXAMPLE: A large, shiny object lay *on the ground*.
<u>On the ground lay a large, shiny object.</u>

1. The person who has committed the murder is *here, in this very room*.

_____

2. Some of the most prominent citizens of the town were *among those collaborating with the army of occupation*.

_____

3. The little store where I buy my groceries is *around the corner*.

_____

4. You will see such beautiful flowers *nowhere else*.

_____

5. Books, magazines, newspapers were piled *on the desk*.

_____

6. Many varieties of mushrooms can be found *in these woods*.

_____

7. The peak of the great mountain loomed *far off in the distance*.

_____

8. The decisive battle of the war was fought *on this very ground*.

_____

9. A large tatoo of an eagle was *on his left arm*.

_____

7-5
-*LY* ADVERBS (1)

Adverbs of manner are formed by adding -**ly** to adjectives. When changing adjectives to adverbs, keep in mind that:

1. final **y** becomes **i** before -**ly**—**happily, merrily** (but **gayly** or **gaily**)
2. final **e** is kept before -**ly**—**fortunately, sincerely** (but **wholly, truly**)
3. **le** preceded by a consonant is dropped before -**ly**—**simply, idly**
4. both -**ic** and -**ical** become -**ically**—**basically, geographically** (*but* **publicly**)

Change the following adjectives to -*ly* adverbs. Make whatever spelling changes are necessary. (Keep in mind that -*ly* added to an adjective already ending in *l* requires two *l*'s.)

busy _____   possible _____

accidental _____   potential _____

cheerful _____   true _____

cruel _____   occasional _____

sensible _____   hygienic _____

excessive _____   evident _____

favorable _____   public _____

sincere _____   simple _____

extreme _____   dry _____

whole _____   total _____

full _____   historic _____

customary _____   skillful _____

equal _____   easy _____

necessary _____   unfortunate _____

systematic _____

7-6
-LY ADVERBS (2)

Change each sentence so that the adjective becomes an **-ly** adverb of manner.

EXAMPLE: a. She always dresses in a simple manner.
                She always dresses simply.

            b. She is a careless typist.
                She types carelessly.

            c. He gave a prompt answer.
                He answered promptly.

1. She walks in an awkward manner.

_____

2. He is a brave fighter.

_____

3. The audience applauded in an enthusiastic manner.

_____

4. He was treated in a cruel way.

_____

5. She is a shameless liar.

_____

6. He spoke in a modest but convincing manner.

_____

7. She replied in an angry manner.

_____

8. He addressed the professor in a respectful manner.

_____

9. He expressed his views in a simple and sincere manner.

_____

10. The money was divided in an equal manner among all the children.

_____

11. He is a careful driver.

_____

7-7
ADVERBS vs. ADJECTIVES

With certain verbs, adjective forms may be used rather than adverbs. These adjective forms express a state rather than manner. Verbs taking adjectives are linking verbs like **be, seem, look, appear, become,** and verbs of the senses (**smell, taste, feel**) when they refer back to the subject. In addition, a number of other verbs combine with adjectives to form idiomatic expressions—**grow worse, prove wrong, blow open, break loose, play fair, open wide, hold tight, go wrong, sound right.**

Use the proper form of the word in parentheses.

EXAMPLE: a. That man looks (desperate).

That man looks desperate. (**desperate** refers to the subject—(a **desperate** man)

b. He was looking (desperate) for the wallet he had lost.

He was looking desperately for the wallet he had lost. (**desperately** expresses manner in relation to the transitive verb **look.**)

1. These eggs seem (fresh).

_____

2. This coffee was (fresh) made.

_____

3. The baby's skin feels very (smooth).

_____

4. I don't feel (good) today. My head hurts.[3]

_____

[3]After the verb **feel, well** refers to one's physical health, **good** and **bad** to one's emotional state (formal usage).

5. I feel (bad) about his losing his job.[3]

_____

6. He was (bad) hurt in the accident.

_____

7. He appears (uneasy) about something.

_____

8. He looked about him (uneasy).

_____

9. They don't play (fair).

_____

10. Do you think he was treated (fair)?

_____

11. I wonder what could have gone (wrong)?

_____

12. He was (wrong) accused of the murder.

_____

13. He held his head (high) even after defeat.

_____

14. He is (high) regarded in the community.

_____

15. This product is (cheap) made.

_____

16. The dentist asked his patient to open his mouth (wide).

_____

17. The lion broke (loose) from his cage.

_____

18. He becomes very (angry) when he doesn't get his way.

_____

19. The rumor about their divorce proved (false).

_____

20. The machine was repaired yesterday. It is now working (good).

_____

21. The milk tastes (sour).

_____

22. He is (firm) convinced that he is (right).

_____

23. I wish you wouldn't slam the door so (hard).[4]

_____

24. Please don't drive so (fast). The sign says, Drive (Slow).[4]

_____

25. He (slow) turned his head from side to side.

_____

26. His clothes always fit him (perfect).

_____

27. A zoo often smells (bad).

_____

REVIEW OF ADVERBS

A. Arrange the words in the best possible way.

1. has been, extremely, ever since his accident, he, about his driving, careful.

_____

2. hastily, while he was waiting for her, something, wrote, he, on a piece of paper.

_____

3. be, to the post office, to mail the letters, at 5:00 p.m., his office boy, sent.

_____

4. anxiously, from their windows, they, all through the night, watched, for the returning planes.

_____

5. very well, speaks, when he's not tired, English, he.

_____

B. Rewrite the sentences placing the *italicized* words at the beginning of each sentence.

1. She entered the room *so silently* that no one noticed her.

_____

[4]Some adverbs have the same form as adjectives—**hard, fast, slow** (only after certain verbs), **early, late.**

2. The little store where I buy my groceries is *around the corner*.

_____

3. I will consent to see him *only if he apologizes*.

_____

4. You will see such beautiful flowers *nowhere else*.

_____

5. His new car is *not only* less expensive than his old one, but it also uses less gasoline.

_____

C. Rewrite, changing the adjectives to adverbs.

accidental _____   equal _____

sensible _____   true _____

excessive _____   evident _____

sincere _____   total _____

whole _____   historic _____

customary _____   angry _____

enthusiastic _____   respectful _____

convincing _____   systematic _____

D. Use the proper form of the word in parentheses.

1. The baby's skin feels very (smooth) _____.

2. He appears (uneasy) _____ about something.

3. I wonder what could have gone (wrong) _____.

4. This product is (cheap) _____ made.

5. His clothes always fit him (perfect) _____.

6. I wish you wouldn't slam the door so (hard) _____.

7. The milk tastes (sour) _____.

8

Prepositions

PREPOSITIONS

FUNCTION: A preposition connects a noun structure to some other word in the sentence. The noun structure may be:

1. *a noun*   The jeweler showed the diamond ring to **his wife.**
2. *a pronoun*   The jeweler showed the diamond ring to **her.**
3. *a gerund phrase*   The jeweler did not object to **showing the diamond ring to her.**
4. *a noun clause*   The jeweler showed the diamond ring to **whoever might be a potential buyer.**

Special functions of prepositional forms:
   1. *part of verb* (verb-preposition combinations)—**keep on** (= continue), **get up** (= awake), **go over** (= review)
   2. *adverb* (mostly place and direction):
      He went **down.** (**Down** is an adverb).
      He went **down** the stairs. (**Down** is a preposition.)
      Some prepositional forms are also used as conjunctions (mostly time):
         I will see you **after** dinner is served. (**After** is a conjunction.)
         I will see you **after** dinner. (**After** is a preposition.)

POSITION: A preposition usually appears before its noun object. A preposition may appear in final position in:

1. *a question*   Which house does he live **in?**
2. *an adjective clause*   There is the house (which) he lives **in.**
3. *a noun clause*   I don't know which house he lives **in.**

FORM: A preposition may be composed of one, two, or three parts.

1. *one part*   of, on, at, by, from
2. *two parts*   because of, according to, apart from, as for
3. *three parts*   by means of, with reference to, on account of, in regard to

---

PREPOSITIONAL PHRASES

FUNCTION:

1. *adverbial*   sit **under a tree**, leave **at nine o'clock**
2. *adjectival*   the subway **under the street**, the meeting **at nine o'clock**
3. *nominal (as a "prepositional object" of a verb)*—dispose **of the goods**, wait **for John.**

POSITION: An adjectival prepositional phrase appears after the noun it modifies (the student **in the back row**). A nominal phrase appears after a verb (listen **to your parents**). An adverbial phrase has three possible positions:

1. *initial*   **In spite of her handicap,** the blind girl did well in school.
2. *mid*   The blind girl, **in spite of her handicap,** did well in school.
3. *final*   The blind girl did well in school **in spite of her handicap.**

It is possible to have a sequence of prepositional phrases:

1. *adverbial*   The members met **in Paris on July 16.**
2. *adjectival*   The meeting **of the members in Paris on July 16.**

8-1

PREPOSITIONS OF TIME

1.   One point in time—**on** (with *days*—may be omitted informally);
                        at (with *noon, night, midnight;* with the *time of day*);
                        in (with *other parts of the day*, with *months*, with *years*, with *seasons*).
2.   Extended time—**since, for** (sometimes omitted informally with a definite quantity), **by, from–to** (or **from–until**), **during, (with)in.**

Supply the required preposition of time.

1.   They are getting married _____ Friday

_____ six o'clock _____ the evening.

2.   Exactly _____ midnight we were awakened by the shrill sound of the air raid sirens.

3.   The reception will be _____ Sunday

_____ four _____ the afternoon.

4.   Spring begins _____ March 21, summer

_____ June 21, autumn _____

Sept. 22, and winter _____ December 22.

5.   They seldom travel _____ the winter.

6. The event took place _____ August.

7. He came to this country _____ August 5, 1968.

8. He came to this country _____ 1968.

9. Daffodils usually bloom _____ late March.

10. World War Two lasted _____ 1939

_____ 1945.

11. They say that _____ the spring a young man's fancy fondly
turns to thoughts of love.

12. He has not felt well _____ a long time, ever

_____ his accident.

13. He has been away from home _____ two weeks.

14. They never go out _____ night

_____ the week.

15. _____ the storm, all the lights were out

_____ several hours.

16. We'll be ready to leave _____ an hour from now.

17. We'll have finished all the work _____ the time you get
here.

18. He has been away from home _____ January 12.

19. _____ tomorrow, the worst of the storm should be over.

20. Recently he has been having trouble getting to sleep _____
night.

21. The temperature is below zero. _____ a few hours the pond
should be frozen over.

8-2

PREPOSITIONS OF PLACE

1. The point itself—**in, inside** (for something contained), **on** (the surface), **at** (some
   area in general; *also* **at the table, desk**)
2. Higher than a point—**over** (generally), **above** (directly).
3. Lower than a point—**under** (generally), **underneath** (close under), **beneath, below**
   (directly).
4. Neighboring the point—**near, by, next to, between, among, opposite.**

For an address, **on** is used for the street (**on Main Street**), and **at** is used if the street
number is included (**at 220 Main Street**).

Supply the required preposition of place.

1. I'll meet you _____ the Statler Hotel.

2. If you want to reach that shelf you'd better stand _____ a chair.

3. You will find some stamps _____ the middle drawer of the desk.

4. We are still living _____ Bedford Avenue. We used to live _____ 450 Bedford Avenue, but now we live _____ 631 Bedford Avenue.

5. This apartment is 10D; 11D is the apartment directly _____ us.

6. _____ the box were the earrings she thought she had lost.

7. Some of the most expensive stores _____ New York are _____ Fifth Avenue.

8. _____ the front page of the newspaper are the most important stories of the day.

9. Please play _____ the house. It's too cold outside.

10. When you are sitting _____ the table for dinner, don't put your elbows _____ the table.

11. There is no one _____ the world who can help me now.

12. The boy hid the money _____ a rock _____ the garden.

13. A subterranean river runs _____ the ground.

14. The tax office is _____ the second floor.

15. A submarine operates _____ the surface of the water.

16. We'll wait for you _____ the lobby of the hotel.

17. He saw a dollar bill lying _____ the sidewalk.

18. Turn left _____ the next intersection.

19. The pupils were busy writing some exercises _____ their desks.

20. They arrived _____ the United States last week.[1]

21. The plane arrived _____ the airport two hours late.[1]

[1]**Arrive in** is used for a larger geographical area such as a country. **Arrive at** is used for a smaller area such as a building, a station, an airport. With cities or towns, **arrive in** is far more common than **arrive at**.

8-3
PREPOSITIONAL OBJECTS

Some verbs take objects that are introduced by prepositions.

at	glance, laugh, look, marvel, rejoice, shudder, smile, stare
of	approve, beware, consist, despair, smell
of *or* **about**	boast, dream, speak, talk, think
for	call, hope, long, look, mourn, pray, wait, watch, wish

Supply the preposition required after each verb.

1. He kept glancing impatiently _____ his watch.

2. We should beware _____ those who flatter.

3. The room smells _____ paint.

4. The old man spoke _____ the hair-raising experiences he had had as a spy.

5. Listen! Do you hear someone calling _____ help?

6. Don't embarrass him by laughing _____ his mistakes in English.

7. Sometimes I despair _____ ever finishing this job.

8. Those people long _____ the day their country will be free again.

9. Don't stare _____ her; just look _____ her quickly.

10. We rejoiced _____ his miraculous escape.

11. Water consists _____ hydrogen and oxygen.

12. Lately he has been thinking _____ her a great deal.

13. Everyone shuddered _____ the tale of terror he told.

14. Her parents disapprove _____ her staying out late at night.

15. I'll wait _____ you here.

16. He has always dreamed _____ going to England.

17. I can't find my ring. I've looked _____ it everywhere.

18. He's forever boasting _____ his brave exploits in the last war.

19. She mourned _____ her deceased husband for a long time.

20. We've always marveled ⎯⎯⎯⎯⎯⎯⎯⎯⎯⎯⎯⎯ her ability to get along with all kinds of people.

21. I can't talk ⎯⎯⎯⎯⎯⎯⎯⎯⎯⎯⎯⎯ things I don't understand.

---

to	allude, aspire, conform, consent, listen, object, point, reply, resort, respond, subscribe, yield
(up)on	count, decide, depend, feed, impose, insist, plan, reflect, rely
with	associate, consult, cope, deal, dispense, interfere, join, meddle, part, side, unite, vie
from	abstain, cease, deviate, differ, dissent, emerge, escape, flee, recover, retire, shrink

Supply the preposition required after each verb.

1. We're counting ⎯⎯⎯⎯⎯⎯⎯⎯⎯⎯⎯ you not to interfere

   ⎯⎯⎯⎯⎯⎯⎯⎯⎯⎯⎯ the project.

2. He mentioned the subject once, but he has never alluded

   ⎯⎯⎯⎯⎯⎯⎯⎯⎯⎯⎯ it again.

3. The sun was reflecting ⎯⎯⎯⎯⎯⎯⎯⎯⎯⎯⎯ his windshield and making it difficult to drive.

4. Let's dispense ⎯⎯⎯⎯⎯⎯⎯⎯⎯⎯⎯ all formalities and abstain

   ⎯⎯⎯⎯⎯⎯⎯⎯⎯⎯⎯ taking sides in this dispute.

5. Some prisoners had escaped ⎯⎯⎯⎯⎯⎯⎯⎯⎯⎯⎯ prison and were fleeing

   ⎯⎯⎯⎯⎯⎯⎯⎯⎯⎯⎯ their pursuers.

6. Many young people today refuse to conform ⎯⎯⎯⎯⎯⎯⎯⎯⎯⎯⎯ society's regulations.

7. A severe fine was imposed ⎯⎯⎯⎯⎯⎯⎯⎯⎯⎯⎯ him for his improper behavior in the courtroom.

8. He expects to retire ⎯⎯⎯⎯⎯⎯⎯⎯⎯⎯⎯ his job in a few months.

9. At first her parents objected ⎯⎯⎯⎯⎯⎯⎯⎯⎯⎯⎯ the young man, but they

   finally consented ⎯⎯⎯⎯⎯⎯⎯⎯⎯⎯⎯ their marriage.

10. I insist ⎯⎯⎯⎯⎯⎯⎯⎯⎯⎯⎯ seeing him at once.

11. After years of imprisonment, he was finally reunited ⎯⎯⎯⎯⎯⎯⎯⎯⎯⎯⎯ his family.

12. He never seems to be listening ⎯⎯⎯⎯⎯⎯⎯⎯⎯⎯⎯ what people say to him.

13. He is so sensitive that he cannot cope ⎯⎯⎯⎯⎯⎯⎯⎯⎯⎯⎯ all his problems.

14. A situation arose which they had not planned ⎯⎯⎯⎯⎯⎯⎯⎯⎯⎯⎯ .

15. When people are desparate, they may resort ⎯⎯⎯⎯⎯⎯⎯⎯⎯⎯⎯ violence.

16. He subscribed _____ many magazines.

17. The outcome of the experiment depends _____ several factors.

18. This new batch of cookies differs somewhat _____ the first one.

---

in	believe, confide, consist, deal, delight, end, engage, excel, indulge, participate, persevere, result, succeed
for *or* against	contend, declare, demonstrate, fight, strike, strive, vote
against	immunize, plot, rebel, struggle
into	transform, turn
over	reign, rule

Supply the preposition required after each verb.

1. He doesn't believe _____ anything at all.

2. The young people today are demonstrating _____ war and _____ peace.

3. Someone who plots _____ his own country is a traitor.

4. That dictator rules _____ the people with an iron hand.

5. She has always confided _____ her husband.

6. They have transformed that old house _____ an antique shop.

7. Which candidate are you voting _____?

8. He deals only _____ modern paintings.

9. Men have often had to fight _____ freedom.

10. Her line has been busy for a long time, but we've finally succeeded _____ reaching her.

11. The whole project ended _____ failure.

12. Vaccines are available to immunize people _____ many diseases.

13. He excels _____ all sports.

14. Her son never liked to participate _____ class discussions.

15. If you persevere _____ your studies you are bound to succeed.

16. We must continue to struggle _____ poverty.

17. Her husband's drinking problem can only result _____ tragedy for the family.

VERBS WITH DIRECT OBJECTS
AND PREPOSITIONAL OBJECTS

A verb may have both a direct object and a prepositional object.

She always needs to remind **her husband of his dental appointments.**

Only the direct object becomes the subject of the passive.

The store was robbed of $500 last night.
(*active*—Someone robbed **the store** of $500 last night).

Second Object with:	
of	accuse, convict, deprive, persuade, rob, suspect
of *or* **about**	advise, convince, remind, warn
about	ask, question
from	borrow, buy, collect, conceal, distinguish, hide, keep, protect, rescue, stop
on	base, inflict
with	burden, connect, entrust, help, provide
for	ask, blame, condemn, forgive, reprimand, reproach, substitute

Supply the required preposition.

1. The man accused his partner ———————————— cheating.

2. She suspects her husband ———————————— infidelity but she cannot prove it.

3. We'll have to borrow some money ———————————— the bank to pay for our new car.

4. She reproached her friend ———————————— not having told her sooner.

5. I don't wish to burden you ———————————— all my difficulties.

6. I forgot to ask the doctor ———————————— the medication I should take.

7. I cannot distinguish one twin ———————————— the other.

8. Motorcyclists are required to wear helmets to protect their heads

   ———————————— serious injury.

9. He cannot be persuaded ———————————— the truth of that statement.

10. It took a few days before they were able to rescue the men

    ———————————— the mine that had caved in.

11. He was convicted ———————————— a crime he had not committed.

12. Something is wrong; I'm convinced _____ it.

13. Money was collected _____ the employees to buy a gift for the girl who was getting married.

14. He has already been warned _____ the danger of lung cancer.

15. He was blamed _____ not taking the proper precautions against fire hazards.

16. Everyone who is connected _____ the arrested gambler is being questioned by the police.

17. Oleomargarine may be substituted _____ butter in this recipe.

18. The American Constitution guarantees that no one shall be deprived

    _____ life, liberty, or the pursuit of happiness.

19. The punishment which was inflicted _____ him was too severe.

20. You must get a good lawyer to advise you _____ your rights in this matter.

8-5
INDIRECT OBJECTS WITH OR WITHOUT *TO*

Some indirect objects may appear without a preposition before the direct object, or they may appear in a **to** phrase after the direct object.

> He sent his wife some flowers.
> *or* He sent some flowers to his wife.
> She gave the cashier the money.
> *or* She gave the money to the cashier.[2]

Indirect objects that may be expressed with or without **to** follow verbs such as **bring, give, hand, lend, pay, promise, sell, send, show, teach, write.**

Other indirect objects may be used only in a **to** phrase after the direct object.

> She explained the lesson to the class.
> He described his home town to us.
> The doctor recommended a heart specialist to his patient.
> Can you suggest a good dentist to me?

Additional verbs followed only by **to** indirect objects are **announce, demonstrate, introduce, mention, point out, prove, say, speak.**

---

[2]A few indirect objects require a **for** phrase after the direct object instead of a **to** phrase—**He made (or bought, built, found, got) a bookcase for his daughter.**

Wherever possible, change the **to** indirect object to the form without **to**.

EXAMPLE: a.   She gave some food to the dog.
                 <u>She gave the dog some food.</u>

            b.   The university dedicated the new building to its former president.
                 <u>(*no change possible*)</u>

1.   Please bring the newspaper to me.

   _____

2.   Let me describe the scene to you.

   _____

3.   He handed the money to the salesclerk.

   _____

4.   We plan to sell our house to them.

   _____

5.   You must explain all this to the judge.

   _____

6.   The girl lent her new typewriter to her friend.

   _____

7.   She is teaching geography to the students.

   _____

8.   Don't mention this matter to your friends.

   _____

9.   He had time to speak only a few words to his children.

   _____

10.   The speaker said a few things to me in private.[3]

    _____

11.   Next time I will write a longer letter to you.

    _____

12.   I must recommend a wonderful restaurant to you.

    _____

[3]After **say,** only the **to** indirect object is used—He said nothing **to me** at that time. After **tell,** the indirect object without **to** is more common—He told **me** nothing at that time.

13.   May I suggest something to you?

_____

14.   We gave it to her.[4]

_____

15.   He told the story to his brother.

_____

16.   He said something to his brother.

_____

17.   Can you recommend a good grammar book to us?

_____

18.   Please explain the meaning of this word to me.

_____

8-6
PREPOSITIONS AFTER ADJECTIVES

Many adjectives are followed by prepositions.

from	absent, different, distinct, remote
for	enough, fit, good, grateful, necessary, responsible
in	deficient, proficient, successful
with	compatible, consistent, content, gentle, patient
(up)on	dependent, intent
about	careful (*or* of), enthusiastic (*or* over), happy
of	afraid, aware, certain, conscious, critical, deserving, desirous, envious, fearful, fond, full, glad, guilty, ignorant, innocent, jealous, positive, proud, thoughtful, tolerant, worthy
to	acceptable, adjacent, attentive, beneficial, detrimental, essential, faithful, friendly, generous, hostile, inferior, kind, obedient, painful, partial, polite, preferable, rude, similar

Use the required preposition after each adjective.

1.   He is frequently absent _____ school because of illness.

2.   All that equipment is not necessary _____ our experiment.

3.   He is very proficient _____ English, but very deficient

_____ mathematics.

[4]If both objects are personal pronouns, American usage permits only the **to** indirect object.

4. We'll have to be content _____ the few supplies we have.

5. The young man left home because he no longer wanted to be dependent

   _____ his parents.

6. He was quite aware _____ the appeal he had for women.

7. That proposal is not acceptable _____ our company.

8. He has always been faithful _____ his wife.

9. He is quite different _____ his brother.[5]

10. We're very grateful to you _____ all your help.

11. He has never been successful _____ anything he has undertaken.

12. He's very critical _____ everyone but himself.

13. How thoughtful _____ you to send flowers to the old lady in the hospital.

14. The cemetery is adjacent _____ the church.

15. Too much smoking or drinking is detrimental _____ the health.

16. Is the paper bag strong enough _____ this carton of milk?

17. Although he's a stern, gruff man, he's very gentle _____ children.

18. He's not enthusiastic _____ his new job.

19. She's very fond _____ young children.

20. He is very attentive _____ all the details of his work.

21. The jury decided the defendant was guilty _____ the murder he was accused of.

22. She is responsible _____ all the supplies that are distributed.

23. He always tries to be polite _____ his elders.

24. She's very jealous _____ the attention her younger sister gets.

25. She has always felt inferior _____ her sister.

26. I'm proud _____ the way you behaved in that difficult situation.

27. You must be very careful _____ what you say to him.

[5]The conjunction **than** may also be heard informally after **different.**

8-7
PREPOSITIONS AFTER PARTICIPIAL ADJECTIVES

Many **-ed** participial adjectives are followed by prepositions, usually **in, to, with, at, about** or **over, by, of.**

> I'm tired of his never-ending complaints.
> They have been blessed with many children.
> We are alarmed at (or by) the way the children have been behaving recently.

At or **by** frequently follows **-ed** participial adjectives expressing emotion. **By** after **-ed** adjectives usually strengthens the passive force of these participial forms.

Use the required preposition. In some cases two prepositions are possible.

1. He was so absorbed _____ the work he was doing that he didn't notice our entrance into the room.

2. I'm well acquainted _____ the situation you're referring to.

3. Late in life he was afflicted _____ a terrible disease.

4. I'm not ashamed _____ anything I've done.

5. Astonished _____ what he saw, he stood rooted to the spot.

6. Water is composed _____ hydrogen and oxygen.

7. I'm quite concerned _____ the health of my wife.

8. He is endowed _____ very great gifts.

9. Embarrassed _____ the many compliments he was receiving, the explorer began to wish he could leave the room.

10. We're all impressed _____ your great knowledge of the subject.

11. I'm interested _____ buying a diamond ring for my wife.

12. Pleased _____ the impression he was making, he began to tell about another one of his adventures.

13. Because of the way his wife has behaved, he is disillusioned

    _____ all women.

14. We were all shocked _____ the way they had been treating the children.

15. He's satisfied _____ the car he has just bought.

16. That rock star has become accustomed _____ receiving many compliments.

VERB-PREPOSITION COMBINATIONS (1)

Many idioms consist of common one-syllable verbs plus prepositions.

bring	about		*cause*	give	up		*surrender, relinquish*
	up		*raise a subject,*		out		*distribute*
			raise a child	go	over	NS	*review, rehearse*
call	up		*telephone*		with	NS	*date*
	(up)on	NS[6]	*visit*	grow	up	NS	*mature*
	off		*cancel*	hand	in		*submit*
					down		*transmit*
come	up	NS	*arise*	hold	up		*rob*
do	without	NS	*sacrifice,*		down		*suppress*
			not need				
get	up	NS	*wake up, awake*				
	over	NS	*recover from*				

Use the appropriate prepositional form.

1. The soldiers gave _____ (surrendered) after a hard battle.

2. I wonder what brought _____ (caused) his strange behavior?

3. The meeting has been called _____ (canceled) because some of the members are ill.

4. He feels that he can do _____ (not need) many of the luxuries he now has.

5. A man was giving _____ (distributing) leaflets at the entrance to the hall.

6. Jane is going _____ (dating) a very fine young man now.

7. The man who held _____ (robbed) the bank was caught soon after.

8. This question has been brought _____ (raised) again and again at the committee meeetings.

9. Call _____ (telephone) your friend and invite him to come with us.

10. He doesn't like to get _____ (awake) while it's still dark.

11. Let's go _____ (review) the next lesson together.

12. This ring has been handed _____ (transmitted) from generation to generation.

13. He is being brought _____ (raised) to be a gentleman.

[6]NS = nonseparable. See exercise 8-11.

14. A problem has come _____ (arisen) that requires our immediate attention.

15. I can't seem to get _____ (recover from) this cold.

16. All applications should be handed _____ (submitted) right away.

17. These people are too proud and independent to be held

_____ (suppressed) for long.

18. A good traveling salesman calls _____ (visits) all his customers as often as he can.

8-9
VERB-PREPOSITION COMBINATIONS (2)

keep	on	NS	*continue*	put	off		*postpone*
	off	NS	*refrain from going on*		on		*don (clothes)*
look	after	NS	*take care of*		out		*extinguish*
	up		*search for information*	run	across	NS	*meet or find by chance (also come across)*
make	out		*understand*		over	NS	*(get) hit by a car*
	up	NS	*become reconciled, invent*	take	after	NS	*resemble*
pass	out		*distribute*		over		*assume control*
		NS	*faint*		up		*consider, discuss*
pick	out		*select*		off		*remove (clothes)*
	up		*come to get*	turn	down		*reject*
					off		*stop some kind of power*
					on		*start some kind of power*
					up	NS	*appear*

Use the appropriate prepositional form.

1. You can look _____ (search for) the information you want in any encyclopedia.

2. If we don't get more air in this room, I'll pass _____ (faint) from the heat.

3. They couldn't have picked _____ (selected) a better site for the home they are planning to build.

4. No smoking is allowed here. Please put _____ (extinguish) your cigarette.

5. This intersection near the school is very dangerous. Two children have been run

_____ (hit by cars) here.

6. There are several more questions we must take _____ (consider) before we adjourn the meeting.

7. As soon as he entered the house he turned _____ (stopped the electricity) the porch light and turned _____ (start the electricity) the hall light.

8. You will be criticized if you don't turn _____ (appear) for that meeting.

9. Anyone who keeps _____ (continues) making the same mistakes is not very intelligent.

10. I can't make _____ (understand) whether this letter is a *p* or a *q*.

11. Never put _____ (postpone) for tomorrow what you can do today.

12. The girl is very beautiful; she takes _____ (resembles) her mother.

13. She turned _____ (rejected) his offer of marriage.

14. Can't you see that the sign says, "Keep _____ (refrain from going on) the grass?

15. Now that they're divorced, who is looking _____ (taking care of) the children?

16. They had a bitter quarrel, and they never made _____ (became reconciled) after that.

17. He is putting _____ (donning) his oldest clothes to paint the house.

18. While she was cleaning the attic she ran _____ (found by chance) some letters she thought she had destroyed years ago.

19. During the revolution, the rebels took _____ (assumed control of) all the radio stations.

20. All the test papers have already been passed _____ (distributed).

21. The laundryman will pick _____ (come to get) the laundry in the morning.

8-10
VERB-PREPOSITION COMBINATIONS (3) (REVIEW)

Use the verb-preposition combination that is the equivalent of the word(s) in parentheses.

1. The soldiers refused to _____ (surrender).

2. He was _____ (raised) in a tiny village.

3. I shall be very pleased to have you _____ (visit) me.

4. I hope the football game won't have to be _____ (canceled) because of the rainy weather.

5. We need to provide for any unexpected difficulties that might

   _____ (arise).

6. He was able to _____ (submit) his report before it was actually due.

7. In an unlimited monarchy, the ruling power is _____ (transmitted) to someone in the royal family.

8. Crime in the streets is getting so bad that a thief will _____ (rob) a person in broad daylight.

9. If you _____ (continue) spending money like that, you'll soon have none left.

10. He is the kind of person who _____ (appears) when he is least expected.

11. Those stories he _____ (invents) about his past exploits are delightful.

12. The tie he has _____ (selected) goes very well with his suit.

13. A procrastinator likes to _____ (postpone) doing the things that should be done right away.

14. We _____ (remove) our coats and hats when we enter a house.

15. The prepositions are being _____ (considered) this week.

16. Many young Americans do not live with their parents after they

   _____ (mature).

8-11
SEPARABLE VERBS

A number of verb-preposition combinations permit a short object to come between their two parts.

He called up *his wife.*
or He called *his wife* up.

If the object is a personal pronoun, it must come between the two parts of the verb.

He called *her* up.

With other verb-preposition combinations, the object appears only after the prepositional form.

He'll call on ***his new customers*** tomorrow.

He'll call on ***them*** tomorrow.

These nonseparable verbs have been marked NS in the preceding exercises (Exercises 8-8 and 8-9). The other verbs listed there are separable if they are transitive.

Use the required pronoun and the proper form of the verb-preposition combination.

EXAMPLE: a. Aren't you going to *the meeting?* No, they've ___called___ ___it___ ___off___(cancelled) (**Call off** is a separable verb.)

          b. *These lessons* are difficult. Let's ___go___ ___over___ ___them___ (review) together. (**Go over** is a nonseparable verb.)

1. I'd better see *the doctor* about this infection. I'll _____ _____ _____ (telephone) right away.

2. The typist has had *the flu* for a long time but she has finally _____ _____

    _____ (recovered from) and is back in the office.

3. Aren't they living in *their apartment* on Smith Street? No, they _____ _____

    _____ (relinquished) last year and moved into a large house.

4. Here are *some good books* on the subject. Please _____ _____ _____ (select). (Use **one**)[7]

5. *The articles* are very difficult to learn. We will _____ _____ _____ (consider) next week.

6. Was *their bid for the contract* accepted? No, the company _____ _____

    _____ (rejected) because it was too high.

7. Here's *an interesting article* about your country. I just _____ _____

    _____ (found by chance) in a magazine.

8. How does *this air conditioner* work? I would like to _____ _____ _____ (start)

9. Do you want to get *a car* for your teen-age son? No, he can _____ _____

    _____ (not need) for a while longer. (Use **one**)

10. Here are *your rubbers*. Please _____ _____ _____ (don)

11. *The books* have finally been delivered. We'll _____ _____ _____ (distribute) tomorrow.

12. We can't hold *the meeting* tonight. We'll have to _____ _____ _____ (postpone) until tomorrow.

13. *My new shoes* are hurting me. I'm going to _____ _____ _____ (remove) for a while.

[7]Some pronouns like **one, this, some** may come before or after the prepositional form in a separable verb.

14. Their art teacher had planned *a trip to the museum,* but he had to _____

_____ _____ (cancel) because he became ill.

15. She is very proud of *her children* because she feels she has _____ _____

_____ (raise children) properly.

8-12
VERB-PREPOSITION COMBINATIONS
+ PREPOSITIONAL OBJECTS

Some verb-preposition combinations are followed by prepositional objects.

From the following list, choose the prepositions that are required in the sentences.

catch on to	understand
catch up with	reach, after being behind
drop in on	visit unannounced or informally
drop out of	discontinue (membership, attendance)
get along with	be agreeable, be on good terms
give in to	surrender, yield
go along with	accept
keep up with	maintain the same pace
look down on	consider as inferior
look up to	consider as superior
put up with	tolerate
run out of	exhaust a supply

1. After his illness, the student had a difficult time keeping _____ _____ his studies.

2. Finally, he decided to drop _____ _____ college.

3. We should avoid looking _____ _____ those who are poorer than we are.

4. That proposal seems reasonable. I'll go _____ _____ it.

5. They always seem to drop _____ _____ us at dinner time.

6. I don't think I can put _____ _____ this noise much longer.

7. Let's stop at a gasoline station before we run _____ _____ gas.

8. Everyone looks _____ _____ a great scientist such as Einstein.

9. Go ahead of me. I'll soon catch _____ _____ you.

10. They had to drop _____ _____ the country club because they could no longer afford it.

11. It's very hard to catch _____ _____ jokes in another language.

12. Parents who often give _____ _____ their children will have spoiled children.

13. It's become increasingly hard for that couple to get _____ _____ each other; they've decided to get a divorce.

14. If a family always wants to have as much as a neighbor has, we say that the family is

trying to keep _____ _____ the Joneses.

PASSIVE OF VERB + PREPOSITION COMBINATIONS

Rewrite the following sentences, changing the italicized verb + preposition combinations to the passive voice. Do not use a **by** phrase if the sentence begins with **they** or **people**.

EXAMPLE: a. Their aunt and uncle *brought up* the orphaned children.
   The orphaned children were brought up by their aunt and uncle.
   (Note that the preposition remains with the verb.)

   b. They may *call off* the lecture series if they don't sell enough tickets.
   The lecture series may be called off if they don't sell enough tickets.

1. The campaign workers *were handing out* leaflets at the meeting.

_____

2. The company *turned off* his electricity because he had not paid his bills.

_____

_____

3. The robbers *had disposed of* the stolen goods before the police arrested them.

_____

_____

4. The students *will have handed in* many reports before the end of the year.

_____

_____

5. They *must decide on* a new plan soon.

_____

6. They *held up* our bank last night.

_____

7. People *will make fun of* you if you give such a silly speech.

_____

8. People always *take advantage of* him because he is so naive.

_____

9. We *must take up* that matter at our next meeting.

_____

10. They *blew up* the bridge after they retreated from the enemy.

_____

11. One of the students *is giving out* the examination papers.

_____

12. They *turned down* the bid because it was too high.

_____

13. Her aunt *is taking care of* her.

_____

14. They *will operate on* him tomorrow.

_____

15. People *have* really *taken notice of* him since he published his book.

_____

8-14
PHRASAL PREPOSITIONS

Prepositions may consist of two or three parts.

1. Two parts—**because of, along with, according to, apart from, owing to, as for, short of, instead of, ahead of, regardless of, contrary to, prior to, subject to.**
2. Three parts—**by way of, in spite of, with (*or* in) regard to, in addition to, in (the) back of (*or* at the back of), by means of, for fear of, for the sake of, on account of, on behalf of, as a result of, in return for, in accordance with, with (*or* in) reference to, in favor of, in connection with, as well as, on the point of.**

A. Supply the missing parts of the phrasal prepositions.

1. The train arrived ahead _____ schedule.

2. Instead _____ listening to his parents, he did just as he pleased.

3. Regardless _____ the consequences, he went ahead with his foolhardy plan.

4. According _____ the newspapers, the President will arrive next week.

5. I don't know what decisions others may make, but as _____ me, give me liberty or give me death.

6. Owing _____ a mistake made by the computer, he received a check for one million dollars.

7. The prices quoted are subject _____ change without notice.

8. Prior _____ his marriage, he had spent money very foolishly.

9. We're very short _____ paper; please order some more immediately.

10. Contrary _____ expectations, the young boy did very well on the examinations.

11. Apart _____ his parents, no one knew that he was planning to leave the country.

12. They were just _____ the point _____ leaving the house when some unexpected visitors arrived.

13. He became paralyzed _____ a result _____ a stroke he had had recently.

14. _____ accordance _____ your request, we are canceling your magazine subscription.

15. All the campaign workers were given handsome gifts _____ return _____ their help.

16. The students sitting _____ the back _____ the room could barely hear the professor.

17. _____ behalf _____ the citizens of his town, the mayor gave his distinguished visitor the keys to the city.

18. _____ the sake _____ peace in the family, she never argued with her husband.

19. Many problems have arisen _____ connection _____ the construction of the new library.

20. The teacher, _____ well _____ the students, was disappointed at the cancellation of their camping trip.

21. _____ means _____ hard work, the young man quickly climbed to the highest position in his department.

22. _____ reference _____ your recent letter, we wish to state that your order is being sent out next week.

B. Use one of the phrasal prepositions given at the beginning of this exercise. In some sentences, there may be choices between phrasal prepositions that have the same meaning.

EXAMPLE: a. <u>Owing to, because of, *or* on account of</u> a breakdown in their computer, the bank had to halt business for a while.

b. <u>In spite of *or* regardless of</u> the heavy rain, they kept driving until they reached their destination.

1. The others can walk if they want to. _____ me, I'll take the bus.

2. Let's use milk in the coffee _____ cream.

3. His success in business was accomplished _____ hard work.

4. _____ your recent letter, we wish to advise you that you may return the damaged merchandise for a full refund.

5. They are flying to Tokyo _____ the North Pole.

6. Everyone at this meeting who is _____ this proposal, please signify by saying "aye."

7. _____ the badly flooded roads, all traffic was diverted to the side streets.

8. _____ your instructions, we are changing some of the specifications for your new house.

9. _____ his client, the lawyer entered a plea of "not guilty by reason of insanity."

10. They plan to continue driving _____ the weatherman's prediction of more snow.

11. _____ statements made by several economists, the rate of unemployment should continue to drop.

12. He is going to a health spa _____ his bad health.

13. The police refused to shoot it out with the hostage taker

    _____ harming the hostages.

14. The students, _____ their teacher, thought that their trip to the museum had been very beneficial.

15 _____ what some people say about his faults, I believe he is a genius.

8-15
PREPOSITIONS OF
CAUSE, CONCESSION, CONDITION, TIME

Prepositional phrases can be the equivalent of adverbial clauses, especially those phrases beginning with **because of, in spite of, in case of, during.**

Change the italicized clauses to prepositional phrases.

EXAMPLE: a. _Because he was careless_, he lost his job.
   Because of his carelessness, he lost his job.

   b. _Although he is blind_, he manages to live a normal life.
   In spite of his blindness (or despite his blindness), he manages to live a normal life.

   c. _If there is an accident_, notify the police at once.
   In case of an accident (or in the event of an accident), notify the police at once.

   d. _While he was young_, he was very poor.
   During his youth, he was very poor.

1. *Because he is selfish*, he has very few friends.

    _____

2. *Although he is young*, he assumes great responsibility.

    _____

3. *If there is a strike*, all production will be halted.

    _____

4. *While they were engaged*, her fiancé always behaved very courteously.

    _____

5. *Because he was injured*, an ambulance had to be called.

    _____

6. *Although they were poor*, they managed to furnish their apartment in good taste.

    _____

7. *Because they were lonely in the city*, they moved back to the country.

    _____

8. *Although he is bad-tempered*, he is really a kind person.

    _____

9. *If there is a cancellation*, we will let you know at once.

    _____

10. He was rewarded *because he was loyal to his king*.

    _____

11. *While there is a strike*, no one can cross the picket line.

    _____

12. *Although she was ill*, she came to work.

    _____

13. *If the weather is bad*, the picnic will be postponed.

    _____

14. *Although he was innocent*, the jury declared him guilty.

    _____

15. *While she was a child*, she was given everything but love.

    _____

Like and **as** often express comparison or manner.

Comparison	*Like his father,* he loves to go hunting and fishing.
	This tea is (as) cold *as* ice. (The first *as* may be omitted in informal English.)
	This chair is not *so* (or *as*) comfortable as that one. (*So* or *as* may be used after a negative.)
Manner	He has always behaved *like* a perfect gentleman.
(may be	But—If a verb follows **gentleman**, formal usage requires the conjunction **as**—
related to	*He has always behaved **as** a gentleman **should*** (*behave*).
comparison)	

Like and **as** (usually **such as**) may be used to cite an example—**Fruits like** (or **such as**) **apples and bananas are often used for dessert.**
The preposition **as** may also occur in many other types of sentences.

He demanded his rights *as* a citizen.

The teacher appointed a student to act *as* monitor until she returned. (**as** = in the capacity of)

In biology, the horse is classified as *as* a mammal.

We regard him *as* the best possible candidate.

Supply **like** or **as.** Follow formal usage.

1. At school, the young prince wanted to be treated _____ everyone else.

2. _____ a young man, he was very energetic and quick.

3. She is not so cooperative _____ her sister is.

4. She is not cooperative _____ her sister.

5. A sick man _____ him shouldn't work so hard.

6. The dictionary defines democracy _____ "government by the people."

7. People used to say that Stalin was as hard _____ steel.

8. Don't ask questions. Please do _____ you are told.

9. She looks just _____ her mother.

10. The rumor spread _____ wildfire throughout the school.

11. He has been described _____ a very honest and loyal official.

12. The men were asked to select the bravest among them

   _____ their leader.

13. Flowers _____ orchids and gardenias grow only in warm climates.

14. She refers to herself _____ the queen of the kitchen.

15. An opportunity _____ this doesn't present itself every day.

16. He is regarded _____ a saint by many of his followers.

17. Sometimes his secretary dresses _____ a movie star.

18. The Vice President must function _____ the head of the government if anything happens to the President.

19. He has a habit of classifying everyone he meets _____ a friend or _____ an enemy.

20. He often acts _____ a man who is not in his right mind.

8-17
PREPOSITIONS
IN ADVERBIAL WORD GROUPS

Prepositions are often used in adverbial word groups. In such adverbials, countable nouns may occur without articles—**for example, by accident, in fact.** Also adjective forms may function as the objects of prepositions—**for good, at first, in general.**

Supply the proper prepositions for each adverbial word group.

1. They had a bitter quarrel about the money. _____ the end, they decided to divide it equally.

2. All these rugs are made _____ hand.

3. He has left the country _____ good. He will never return.

4. He made a few mistakes, but _____ the whole, I think he did a good job.

5. All payments must be made _____ advance.

6. The young boy learned very fast, and _____ due course he became president of the company.

7. Do you think she hurt his feelings _____ purpose?

8. _____ accident she stepped into a deep puddle of water.

9. Surrounded by the enemy _____ all sides, they had no choice but to surrender.

10. _____ chance, do you remember where they live?

11. We'll have to walk. The elevator is _____ order.

12. There will be twenty guests _____ all.

13. He is _____ far the worst student in the class.

14. She has no patience with children _____ all.

15. This package was left here _____ mistake.

16. She loves bargains. She's going to look at some dresses that are

    _____ sale downtown.

17. Several houses in the area are _____ sale.

18. To memorize means to learn _____ heart.

19. His complaint is about the policy of the company _____ gen-

    eral, not about any one person _____ particular.

20. She was on the phone for a long time; _____ the meantime
    her dinner was burning on the stove.

21. _____ the one hand he would like to spend the summer

    writing his book. _____ the other hand, he feels that he
    ought to travel during his vacation.

22. _____ occasion he wonders why he accepted the new job.

    _____ a matter _____ fact, he
    thinks he made a mistake altogether in accepting it.

23. _____ a rule, he goes to bed at 10 o'clock.

    _____ fact, he has rarely gone to bed later than 11 o'clock.

24. The only way to get to that ancient temple in the jungle is

    _____ plane.[8]

REVIEW OF PREPOSITIONS

A. Supply the required preposition.

1. The reception will be _____ Sunday

   _____ four _____ the afternoon.

2. He has been away from home _____ two weeks.

3. We now live _____ 631 Bedford Avenue.

4. When you are sitting _____ the table for dinner, don't put

   your elbows _____ the table.

5. The tax office is _____ the second floor.

[8]**By** is used with most means of transportation—**by bus, by train, by taxi**—*but* **on foot, on horseback.**

6. Some of the most expensive stores _____ New York are

_____ Fifth Avenue.

7. Water consists _____ hydrogen and oxygen.

8. Her parents disapprove _____ her staying out late

_____ night.

9. Let's dispense _____ all formalities and abstain

_____ taking sides in this dispute.

10. Many young people today refuse to conform _____ society's regulations.

11. He never seems to be listening _____ what people say to him.

12. When people are desperate, they may resort _____ violence.

13. The outcome of the experiment depends _____ several factors.

14. She has always confided _____ her husband.

15. Her son never liked to participate _____ class discussions.

16. I cannot distinguish one twin _____ the other.

17. The American Constitution guarantees that no one shall be deprived

_____ life, liberty or the pursuit of happiness.

18. He's very critical _____ everyone but himself.

19. The cemetery is adjacent _____ the church.

20. She is responsible _____ all the supplies that are distributed.

21. Water is composed _____ hydrogen and oxygen.

22. I'm interested _____ buying a diamond ring for my wife.

23. I'm well acquainted _____ the situation you're referring to.

24. He is very proficient _____ English.

25. He was convicted _____ a crime he had not committed.

26. People used to say that Stalin was as hard _____ steel.

27. She looks just _____ her mother.

28. He made a few mistakes, but _____ the whole, I think he did a good job.

29. _____ chance, do you remember where they live?

30. To memorize means to learn _____ heart.

B. Use the pronoun for the italicized words and the proper form of the verb-preposition combination.

1. *These lessons* are difficult. Let's _____ _____ _____ (review) together.

2. The typist has had *the flu* for a long time but she has finally _____ _____ _____ (recovered from) and is back in the office.

3. *The articles* are very difficult to learn. We will _____ _____ _____ (consider) next week.

4. Here are *your rubbers*. Please _____ _____ _____ (don).

5. *The books* have finally been delivered. We'll _____ _____ _____ (distribute) tomorrow.

C. Change the italicized clauses to prepositional phrases.

1. *If there is an accident*, notify the police.

_____

2. *While he was young*, he was very poor.

_____

3. *Because he is selfish*, he has very few friends.

_____

4. *Although they were very poor*, they managed to furnish their apartment in good taste.

_____

5. He was rewarded *because he was loyal to his king*.

_____

D. Rewrite the following sentences, changing the italicized verb + preposition combinations to the passive voice. Do not use a **by** phrase if the sentence begins with **they** or **people**.

1. The campaign workers *were handing out* leaflets at the meeting.

_____

2. People always *take advantage of* him because he is so naive.

_____

3. We *must take up* that matter at our next meeting.

_____

4. They *blew up* the bridge after they retreated from the enemy.

_____

5. They *will operate on* him tomorrow.

_____

Structure Tests

Part 1

Add the required words in the blank spaces. Use only *one word* in a blank. Write an *X* in those blanks where no word is required.

1. She appreciated _____ flowers which had been sent to her.

2. What does hydrogen consist _____?

3. The scissors _____ on the table a moment ago.

4. Most Americans prefer coffee _____ tea.

5. They _____ up their children to respect the law.

6. It's such _____ nice weather that I hate to stay indoors.

7. She doesn't approve _____ smoking.

8. I haven't seen Mary _____ she came to New York.

9. John would rather have a boat _____ a car.

10. All the furniture _____ being moved to another room.

11. We tried to guess _____ might be appointed.

12. We should be loyal to the country _____ live in.

13. I have to go to _____ town today.

14. _____ well she plays the piano!

15. _____ finishes first will win a prize.

16. He is more famous _____ his brother.

17. They had _____ toast for breakfast.

18. Never again _____ I lend him any money.

19. All the students were sitting quietly _____ their desks.

20. Please try _____ this suit to see if it fits.

21. He is studying _____ American history.

22. Not everyone believes _____ superstition.

23. We _____ just sat down to dinner when the telephone rang.

24. We will wait here _____ John comes.

25. Your remark is not relevant _____ the subject.

26. Each of his children _____ getting an expensive gift for Christmas.

27. _____ I see George, he has a cigarette in his mouth.

28. _____ water in this bay is polluted.

29. He's not afraid _____ anyone.

30. Most of his luggage _____ lost on his last trip.

31. _____ is snowing very hard now.

32. The house has _____ entirely destroyed by the fire.

33. He has been having financial trouble, _____ he?

34. The manager isn't here; she must _____ taking a break.

35. Steamboats used to sail along _____ Mississippi River.

36. He is married _____ a beautiful woman.

37. _____ is something wrong with this typewriter.

38. She would _____ met you at the station if she had known you were coming.

39. Your coat is the same _____ mine.

40. We _____ eat in order to survive.

41. He enjoys walking along _____ Fifth Avenue.

42. Are you familiar _____ this type of work?

43. _____ is too much noise in this part of town.

44. He displayed _____ wisdom far beyond his years.

45. There are enough chairs, aren't _____?

46. His father fought in _____ World War II.

47. It's beginning to rain, isn't _____?

48. Flowers _____ orchids and gardenias grow only in warm climates.

49. He went to the fair ————————————————— foot.

50. He tells the same story to ————————————————— will listen.

Part 2

In each group of sentences, *only one sentence is correct.* Put a circle around the letter of the correct sentence.

1. How did the team play?
   a. The whole team played very good.
   b. The whole team played very well.
   c. The whole team played exceptional.

2. Where are my rubbers?
   a. Here they are. Please put them on.
   b. Here they are. Please put on them.
   c. Here they are. Please put them off.

3. Did your club choose a new president?
   a. Yes, we did chose one last week.
   b. Yes, we chose one last week.
   c. Yes, we have chosen one last week.

4. Have they dug the hole for the tree yet?
   a. They digged the hole a few days ago.
   b. They have dug the hole a few days ago.
   c. They dug the hole a few days ago.

5. John is now married.
   a. When he got married?
   b. When did he get married?
   c. When did he get marry?

6. My wife has a new coat.
   a. How much her new coat cost?
   b. How much did her new coat cost?
   c. How much cost her new coat?

7. Which brother is more famous?
   a. John is the most famous of the two brothers.
   b. John is the more famous of the two brothers.
   c. John is most famous of the two brothers.

8. These bananas aren't ripe yet.
   a. You'd better not eat them.
   b. You'd rather not eat them.
   c. You better not to eat them.

9. He's not in his office.
   a. He should be out to lunch.

    b. He would be out to lunch.

    c. He must be out to lunch.

10. When will your wife wear her new dress?

    a. She has already worn it yesterday.

    b. She worn it yesterday.

    c. She wore it yesterday.

11. What caused the machine to fail?

    a. A breaking spring caused all the trouble.

    b. A broken spring caused all the trouble.

    c. A broke spring caused all the trouble.

12. How much money does he have left?

    a. He still has a few money left.

    b. He still has little money left.

    c. He still has a little money left.

13. When did Alice meet her husband?

    a. She met him two years ago.

    b. She met him two years before.

    c. She met him two years since.

14. Can Marie speak English?

    a. Marie doesn't know how to speak English.

    b. Marie doesn't know to speak English.

    c. Marie can't to speak English.

15. How cold was it?

    a. It was such cold night that the lake froze.

    b. It was such a cold night that the lake froze.

    c. It was so cold night that the lake froze.

16. Do you like your new teacher?

    a. Yes, I do, but she gives too many homeworks.

    b. Yes, I do, but she gives too much homeworks.

    c. Yes, I do, but she gives too much homework.

17. Did you buy anything in the new shopping mall?

    a. No, the clothes in the stores there was too expensive.

    b. No, the clothing in the stores there was too expensive.

    c. No, the clothing in the stores there were too expensive.

18. Did you have a good time at the party?

    a. Yes, I enjoyed very much the party.

    b. Yes, I enjoyed very much.

    c. Yes, I enjoyed myself very much.

19. She's very tired.

    a. She's lying down to rest.

    b. She's laying down to rest.

    c. She has laid down to rest.

20. This pen doesn't work well.
    a. Please give me the another one.
    b. Please give me the other one.
    c. Please give me other one.

21. What kind of desserts are ice cream and sherbet?
    a. Ice cream and sherbet are freezing desserts.
    b. Ice cream and sherbet are froze desserts.
    c. Ice cream and sherbet are frozen desserts.

22. What was the weather like this morning?
    a. The sun shone when I left the house.
    b. The sun has shone when I left the house.
    c. The sun was shining when I left the house.

23. Hurry up and sit down.
    a. The play is beginning now.
    b. The play begins now.
    c. The play has began now.

24. What has John been doing lately?
    a. John was writing a book the last time I saw him.
    b. John has written a book the last time I saw him.
    c. John wrote a book the last time I saw him.

25. How long have the Browns lived in New York?
    a. They have lived there since four years.
    b. They have lived there for four years.
    c. They have lived there during four years.

26. When will you return the books to the library?
    a. I'll return them today if I will have time.
    b. I'll return them today if I have time.
    c. I'll return them today if I had time.

27. Who built their house?
    a. They built their house theirselves.
    b. They built their house themselves.
    c. They built their house themself.

28. How does a zoo smell?
    a. A zoo smells very badly.
    b. A zoo smells very bad.
    c. A zoo smells very strongly.

29. Will his money last for the whole trip?
    a. By the time he gets to Paris, he will have spent all his money.
    b. By the time he gets to Paris, he spent all his money.
    c. By the time he gets to Paris, he has spent all his money.

30. We've just finished our work.
    a. When you will finish yours?

    b. When you finish yours?

    c. When will you finish yours?

31. Does your friend enjoy cooking?

    a. Yes, she is very interesting in cooking.

    b. Yes, she is very interested in cooking.

    c. Yes, she is very interest in cooking.

32. Do you like New York?

    a. Yes, every day is something different to see in New York.

    b. Yes, every day are something different to see in New York.

    c. Yes, every day there is something different to see in New York.

33. When do Americans eat lunch?

    a. Most of Americans eat lunch at noon.

    b. Most Americans eat lunch at noon.

    c. The most Americans eat lunch at noon.

34. Where can I find out about that school?

    a. You can get a lot of informations from their catalog.

    b. You can get very many informations from their catalog.

    c. You can get very much information from their catalog.

35. Where would you like to go for your vacation this summer?

    a. If I have money, I would go to Japan.

    b. If I would have money, I would go to Japan.

    c. If I had money, I would go to Japan.

36. What kind of people do you find in this city?

    a. There are many differents kinds of people in this city.

    b. There are many difference kinds of people in this city.

    c. There are many different kinds of people in this city.

37. Do you have many holidays in your country?

    a. Yes, we celebrate in my country many holidays.

    b. Yes, we celebrate many holidays in my country.

    c. Yes, in my country are many holidays celebrated.

38. How big is your home town?

    a. Compared with New York, my home town is very small.

    b. Comparing with New York, my home town is very small.

    c. Compare with New York, my home town is very small.

39. I have a cold.

    a. I mustn't get too close to others people.

    b. I mustn't get too close to other people.

    c. I mustn't get too close to another people.

40. In the past, could a young man choose his own mate?

    a. No, parents used to choose a bride for their son.

    b. No, parents were used to choose a bride for their son.

    c. No, parents used to choosing a bride for their son.

41. When do we pay for the dinner dance?
    a. Everybody have to pay in advance.
    b. Everybody must to pay in advance.
    c. Everybody has to pay in advance.

42. What is your native country?
    a. I was born in Brazil.
    b. I born in Brazil.
    c. I am born in Brazil.

43. Did you have many friends when you were young?
    a. Yes, I still have many friends who I met them in high school.
    b. Yes, I still have many friends whom I met in high school.
    c. Yes, I still have many friends which I met in high school.

44. They didn't arrive on time for the conference.
    a. If their plane hadn't been delayed, they would have arrived on time.
    b. If their plane was not delayed, they would have arrived on time.
    c. If their plane were not delayed, they would have arrived on time.

45. Do you believe in superstition?
    a. No, but there are many people who still believes in it.
    b. No, but there are many people who still believing in it.
    c. No, but there are many people who still believe in it.

46. What was the weather like last night?
    a. Last night, was snowing very hard.
    b. Last night, it was snowing very hard.
    c. Last night, there was snowing very hard.

47. Why did the company turn off his electricity?
    a. The electricity was turned off because he had not paid his bills.
    b. The electricity been turned off because he had not paid his bills.
    c. The electricity has turned off because he had not paid his bills.

48. What is usually found on the front page of that newspaper?
    a. The front page articles in that newspaper usually consist of news about international events.
    b. The front page articles in that newspaper usually consists of news about international events.
    c. The front page articles in that newspaper usually are consisting of news about international events.

49. When will they decide on the new plan?
    a. The members of the committee must to decide next week.
    b. The members of the committee has to decide next week.
    c. The members of the committee have to decide next week.

50. Did Jane come to class today?
    a. Yes, she came in spite of she had a bad cold.
    b. Yes, she came although she had a bad cold.
    c. Yes, she came despite she had a bad cold.

Appendix

IRREGULAR VERBS

Simple Form of the Verb	Past Tense	Past Participle
abide (*literary*)	abode	abode
arise	arose	arisen
awake	awoke (*sometimes* awaked)	awaked (*Brit.* awoke, awoken)
be	was	been
bear	bore	borne (*meaning* carry)
		born (*meaning* have children)
beat	beat	beaten (*sometimes* beat)
become	became	become
begin	began	begun
behold	beheld	beheld
bend	bent	bent
beseech (*literary*)	besought (*or* beseeched)	besought (*or* beseeched)
bet	bet (*sometimes* betted)	bet (*sometimes* betted)
bid (*meaning* offer money at an auction)	bid	bid
bid (*meaning* ask someone to do something)	bade (*or* bid)	bidden (*or* bid)
bind	bound	bound
bite	bit	bitten (*or* bit)
bleed	bled	bled
blow	blew	blown
break	broke	broken
breed	bred	bred
bring	brought	brought
broadcast	broadcast (*sometimes* broadcasted)	broadcast (*sometimes* broadcasted)
build	built	built
burst	burst	burst
buy	bought	bought
cast	cast	cast
catch	caught	caught

Simple Form of the Verb	Past Tense	Past Participle
chide	chid (*also* chided)	chidden (*also* chided)
choose	chose	chosen
cling	clung	clung
clothe	clad (*literary*) (*also* clothed)	clad (*literary*) (*also* clothed)
come	came	come
cost	cost	cost
creep	crept	crept
dig	dug	dug
dive	dived *or* dove	dived
do	did	done
draw	drew	drawn
dream	dreamt (*more often* dreamed)	dreamt (*more often* dreamed)
drink	drank	drunk
drive	drove	driven
eat	ate	eaten
fall	fell	fallen
feed	fed	fed
feel	felt	felt
fight	fought	fought
find	found	found
flee	fled	fled
fling	flung	flung
fly	flew	flown
forbid	forbade (*or* forbad)	forbidden
forget	forgot	forgotten (*Brit,* forgot)
forsake	forsook	forsaken
freeze	froze	frozen
get	got	gotten (*Brit,* got)
give	gave	given
go	went	gone
grind	ground	ground
grow	grew	grown
hang	{ hung hanged (*meaning* suspended by the neck)	{ hung hanged (*meaning* suspended by the neck)
have	had	had
hear	heard	heard
hide	hid	hidden (*or* hid)
hit	hit	hit
hold	held	held
hurt	hurt	hurt
keep	kept	kept
kneel	knelt (*or* kneeled)	knelt (*or* kneeled)
knit	knit (*or* knitted)	knit (*or* knitted)
know	knew	known
lay	laid	laid
lead	led	led
leap	lept (*more often* leaped)	lept (*more often* leaped)
leave	left	left
lend	lent	lent
let	let	let
lie	lay	lain

Simple Form of the Verb	Past Tense	Past Participle
light	lit (*more often* lighted)	lit (*more often* lighted)
lose	lost	lost
make	made	made
mean	meant	meant
meet	met	met
mislay	mislaid	mislaid
mistake	mistook	mistaken
overcome	overcame	overcome
pay	paid	paid
put	put	put
read	read	read
rend	rent	rent
rid	rid	rid
ride	rode	ridden
ring	rang	rung
rise	rose	risen
run	ran	run
say	said	said
see	saw	seen
seek	sought	sought
sell	sold	sold
send	sent	sent
set	set	set
sew	sewed	sewn (*or* sewed)
shake	shook	shaken
shed	shed	shed
shine (*intrans.*)	shone	shone
shoe	shod (*or* shoed)	shod (*or* shoed, shodden)
shoot	shot	shot
show	showed	shown (*or* showed)
shrink	shrank (*also* shrunk)	shrunk
shut	shut	shut
sing	sang	sung
sink	sank (*also* sunk)	sunk
sit	sat	sat
sleep	slept	slept
slide	slid	slid
sling	slung	slung
slink	slunk	slunk
slit	slit	slit
smite	smote	smitten
speak	spoke	spoken
speed	sped (*or* speeded)	sped (*or* speeded)
spend	spent	spent
spin	spun	spun
spit	spit (*sometimes* spat)	spit (*sometimes* spat)
split	split	split
spread	spread	spread
spring	sprang (*also* sprung)	sprung
stand	stood	stood
steal	stole	stolen
stick	stuck	stuck

Prep. Past. *(handwritten)*

Simple Form of the Verb	Past Tense	Past Participle
sting	stung	stung
stink	stank (*also* stunk)	stunk
strew	strewed	strewn (*or* strewed)
stride	strode	stridden
strike	struck	struck
string	strung	strung
strive	strove (*also* strived)	striven (*also* strived)
swear	swore	sworn
sweep	swept	swept
swim	swam	swum
swing	swung	swung
take	took	taken
teach	taught	taught
tear	tore	torn
tell	told	told
think	thought	thought
thrive	throve (*or* thrived)	thriven (*or* thrived)
throw	threw	thrown
thrust	thrust	thrust
tread (*literary*)	trod	trodden (*or* trod)
undergo	underwent	undergone
understand	understood	understood
wake	woke (*sometimes* waked)	waked (*Brit.* woke, woken)
wear	wore	worn
weave	wove	woven
weep	wept	wept
win	won	won
wind	wound	wound
withdraw	withdrew	withdrawn
withhold	withheld	withheld
withstand	withstood	withstood
wring	wrung	wrung
write	wrote	written

stinging, stinking (handwritten annotation)